early texas homes

early texas homes

By

DOROTHY KENDALL BRACKEN

and

MAURINE WHORTON REDWAY

1956

SOUTHERN METHODIST UNIVERSITY PRESS: DALLAS

Library of Congress Catalog Card Number: 56-12565

Third printing, 1964

PRINTED IN THE UNITED STATES OF AMERICA AT DALLAS, TEXAS

To
CLIFFORD BRACKEN

Whose enthusiasm, patience, and assistance
made the long quest for early Texas homes
a pleasant adventure

Preface

IN THIS BOOK the reader will visit representative houses built in Texas before and, in a few instances, during the Civil War. The text includes short descriptions of the houses and of their environs, historical high points, biographical data on builders or occupants, and other relevant information. These brief sketches will, it is hoped, serve as guides for excursions into further reading, observation, and travel. They do not purport to add up to either a social or an economic history of Texas; neither do they represent an exhaustive survey of all ante-bellum homes extant in Texas. Nor is there attempted in these pages any technical discourse on Texas architecture.

Two aims—to stimulate interest in historic homes in Texas and to encourage movements to preserve them and their history for posterity—have led the writers into many nooks and crannies of the Lone Star state. Since not all areas of Texas were permanently settled before the Civil War, most of the ante-bellum homes in this collection are found north and south of the Old San Antonio Road.

The examples included have been limited to houses which were built wholly or partly before 1865, which are easily accessible, which are well preserved or which show good potentialities for repair and restoration, and which are distinctive in their design or history. Not every Texas ante-bellum house which met all these criteria could be covered, however—there are obviously physical limitations on the size of a volume of this type.

Authorities disagree regarding the facts on some ante-bellum homes. Disparities in dates and names occur in various historical sources. The authors have used their best judgment in selecting the information presented, but are aware that other versions of particular data exist and may have equal claim to accuracy.

As houses are expendable, it is inevitable that structures and grounds will not remain forever as they are described herein. For example, "Catalpa Villa" in Jefferson was torn down after the pages containing its picture and description had gone to press. But it may be hoped that more and more attention will be given to the importance of preserving the homes that remain.

DOROTHY KENDALL BRACKEN
MAURINE WHORTON REDWAY

Dallas, Texas
September, 1956

Acknowledgments

MATERIAL for this book was collected over a period of years through travel, personal interviews, correspondence, and research into primary and secondary sources. The authors are, therefore, indebted to several groups of people, to various institutions and organizations, and to many individuals.

We are, first of all, grateful to those writers living and dead whose recorded accounts of Texas history have been of immense value. We owe a debt of gratitude to those persons all over Texas who were kind enough to answer questionnaires and letters of inquiry concerning historical homes in their immediate vicinity. We are indebted to another group of gracious Texans who answered our knock at their doors with a hospitable "Won't you come in?" and who supplied the visitors with answers to many questions. For useful information we owe thanks to numerous newspaper editors, school officials and teachers, county clerks, city, county, and state librarians, postmasters, chamber of commerce officials, college and university librarians, and officers of historical societies, as well as, specifically, to the Library of Congress and the library of the *Dallas Morning News*.

It would be impossible to name each individual who aided in the compilation of data for this book. For information on the Central Texas area the authors are especially grateful to Hamilton Magruder, Ceylon R. Kidwell, Mrs. Ellen S. Quillin, John P. Pfeiffer, Miss Lucy Waters White, Mrs. Mary Moorman Grant, Miss Mamie McLean, Mrs. R. G. McCorkle, Mrs. Louise Morrison, Mrs. Blanche Peavey, Miss Elsa F. Burg, Miss Grace Huey, Miss Ruth Curry Lawler, Miss Mary Balzer, Mrs. Sebastian Marty, Warren Taylor, Mrs. Max Weinert, Mrs. Edgar H. Lannom, Mrs. Hazel Tegener, Mrs. C. E. Baer, Mrs. T. H. Hollamon, Jr., Mrs. F. E. Hollamon, C. E. Duggan, Mrs. Roy B. Campbell, Mrs. Leonie Pape, Oscar Haas, J. L. Forke, Mrs. Chester B. Allen, Mrs. Stella S. Platz, Mrs. Lena Knispel, Miss Winnie Knispel, Mrs. William A. Wyatt, Sr., James Taylor, William M. Petmecky, Miss Esther L. Mueller, George Jenschke, Udo Henke, Mrs. Dora Nimitz Reagan, Mrs. Ivor W. Young, Mrs. H. S. Jenkins, Lieutenant Colonel J. B. Kemp, Mrs. Sterling C. Robertson, Mr. and Mrs. Dion Van Bibber, Mrs. W. S. Rose, Miss Fannie Ratchford, Mrs. Tula H. Knolle, Mr. and Mrs. Niles Graham, Mr. and Mrs. Raymond M. Hill, Mrs. T. B. Cochran, and Mrs. J. H. Cochran.

We are indebted for information on the Northeast Texas area to Dr. A. L. Long, Mrs. A. A. Hutson, C. C. Lee, Mrs. Dixie Branch, Raiford L. Stripling, W. G. Sharp, Mrs. Jim Carroll, Sam Parker, Henry W. Sublett, Mrs. J. A. McConnell, Mrs. Sara M. Crook Bartlett, Mrs. H. R. Link, Mrs. Forrest Bradberry, H. V. Hamilton, Mrs. Ralph Malone, Mrs. Maude Hunter Carson, G. B. Harrison, Roger N. Conger, Mrs. J. B. Earle, L. B. McCulloch, Mrs. Lilian B. Riley, Mrs. Mary Harrison Eddins, Mrs. Pearl Green Clement, Mrs. Jeff T. Kemp, Mrs. Gladys Peters Austin, Miss Sofie Loftin, Mrs. J. B. Mayfield, R. L. Shelton, Jr., Miss Myrtis Watkins, Mrs. Arch McKay, Mrs. Dan Lester, Mrs. Lues T. Hough, Gilbert N. Campbell, Mrs. G. E. Blain, Mrs. J. H. Scantlin, Mrs. A. C. Ogburn, Mrs. James I. Peters, Mrs. Dolly Key, Mrs. Lois Shepard, Mrs. Mary Alley Carlson, Mrs. Elma Meisenheimer, Mrs. J. F. Lentz, Mrs. W. A. Nunley, Mrs. C. J. Baldwin, Mrs. Leala Anderson, Dr. Richard E. Granbery, Jesse D. Carter, Edward M. Carroll, J. P. Verhalen, Miss Isabelle DeMorse Latimer, Mr. and Mrs. George McAdams, Mrs. Judson Pryor, Pauline Hughes, Mr. and Mrs. H. E. Rawlins, Earle Rawlins, Jr., Herbert Gambrell, Felix McKnight, Stuart McGregor, Mrs. Evelyn Miller Crowell, Mrs. Barry Miller, Mrs. Ruby E. Overton, Charles A. Osborn, Mrs. B. E. Seale, J. A. R. Moseley, Miss Helen Stanley, Miss Siddie Joe Johnson, Mrs. William Johnson (Elizabeth Ann McMurray), and Mrs. Hazel Horn Carroll.

The authors are particularly grateful also, for information on the Southeast Texas area, to Mrs. Myra Prater Clark, Miss Erin Humphrey, Mrs. Elizabeth Newton, Mr. and Mrs. R. H. Whorton, Jr., Mrs. Ethel H. Swain, Mrs. W. O. Carter, Jr., Mrs. Florence Johnson Scott, Mrs. Sam Rankin, Mrs. H. H. Watson, Joe Cross, Violet G. Morgan, Mrs. Edith Evans Glazebrook, Arthur L. Elliott, Mrs. Ameta C. McGloin, Roger B. McGloin, Mrs. John Von Dohlen, Mrs. R. P. Kelly, Mrs. Verna Linburg, Ray D. Torian, Judge J. A. White, Leopold Morris, Mrs. Eloise Callender Watson, Dr. W. W. Sale, Mr. and Mrs. Fred Juergens, Miss Nellie Murphree, Mrs. R. E. Tait, Miss Willene Compton, Mrs. Robert Schaer, Mrs. D. H. Matthews, Oscar A. Seward, Jr., Mrs. Clay L. Seward, Mrs. T. W. Clay, Frank S. Blue, Edwin C. Deckschat, Mrs. William Garber, Miss Marguerite Oberkampf, August Oberkampf, Mrs. Grace Longino, Mrs. Mae Wynne McFarland, Mrs. Marie Lee Phelps, Mrs. Dorothy Cherry Reid, Mac Adams, Miss Ima Hogg, Miss Laura Underwood, Mrs. Ruby E. Jordon, Guy C. Jackson, Jr., Judge F. E. Williams, Mrs. Cortes Pauls, Walter E. Grover, Mrs. Frances Clarke Sayers, Miss Emma Lee, Miss Marie Marburger, Bill Holman, and Mr. and Mrs. Henry Ketchum.

Our sincere thanks for material aid in completing the pictorial part of the volume go to the following: Clifford Bracken, Bill Wood, Jr., Warren O. Clark, Dr. Virginia Blocker, Anne Russell, Richard Carlyon, Borris Studio, Louis James, Ed Harvin, Julian Barnes, T. C. McMullen, Bill Thompson, George H. Seagert, Art Kowert, Pat Baumgartner, Winkelmann Studio, Jerome Elbel, Charles J. Long, Johnnie L. Pasket, the Fox Company, Zintgraff Photographers, Earl B. Moore, F. D. Shakelford, Gordon A. Coyier, Bob Burns, Alfred Ellison, W. Cleigh Nease, Harvey Patteson, Mr. and Mrs. Herman Van Mannon, Pickering Studio, Marvin Hurley, Earl B. Moore, Frank X. Tolbert, the *Texas Almanac,* the *Dallas Morning News,* and numerous chambers of commerce. Special thanks are due Carl Stange, Prints and Photographs Division, Library of Congress, for his painstaking and expert assistance, and the Library of Congress for permission to use pictures from the collection of the Historic American Buildings Survey.

We have been particularly fortunate in the editorial guidance we have received while preparing this book. To Mrs. Margaret L. Hartley of Southern Methodist University Press we wish to express our sincere thanks for her skill and patience.

Contents

early texas homes

Introduction

TEXAS HOMES ARE FRIENDLY and inviting, and have been so from the beginning. In the early days the breezeway of a dog-run house was a good place to throw saddles, shell peas, hang hats—and shelter dogs. The front door with its side lights, seldom covered by blinds, not only gave light to a hall but enabled the occupants to see an approaching stranger so that they might open the door and ask him to come in. The front porch, or veranda, was a pleasant place to spend the evening talking with a neighbor. And the patio of a Mexican-influenced home was ideal for family gatherings and social affairs.

The varied styles of the century-old houses of Texas reflect the many differences in background and temperament among the groups of colonists —Spaniards, Frenchmen, Canary Islanders, Englishmen, Germans—who settled the region during its early years, as well as the differences in topography and climatic conditions to be found in the area, from the treeless plains in the west, where adobe was made of the native clay and straw, to the timber belts of the east, where homes were hand-hewn from virgin forests or fashioned from stone found near by.

Of the earliest homes of Texas, the aboriginal habitations of the Indians, no vestiges remain beyond a few cliff ruins in the mountainous west and the Indian mounds in East Texas. The movable buffalo-hide tepees used by the nomadic Indians and the thatch-covered huts of the agrarian East Texas tribes have long since disappeared.

The oldest remaining dwellings are those of the Spanish colonists, who began by using a primitive *jacal* construction of posts sunk vertically into the ground. The spaces between the logs were chinked with mud. It was common practice among the "reduced Indians" to build crude, temporary houses and corrals of this sort near the missions.

Spanish colonization was sporadic and the colonies were often neglected, but the missions around which they centered reflected, in native materials, something of the Renaissance grandeur of Spain. The porous limestone which was available in the San Antonio region was used not only in the construction of such missions as the queenly Mission San José, but also to fashion houses for the Canary Islanders in San Fernando and the Mexicans in La Villita.

Farther west along the Rio Grande and on the El Paso frontier, the essential building materials were clay and straw, combined into sun-baked adobe bricks. Most of the dwellings were one-room cabins with adobe walls, thatched roofs, and dirt floors. The thick walls furnished effective insulation against the heat; but although they were solid they were without reinforcement, and were vulnerable to the destructive forces of time and weather. Few of these low, earth-built houses remain standing.

During the last years of the waning Spanish empire in Texas, much havoc was wrought by filibusters and revolutionists. On his trip through Spanish Texas in 1806, Zebulon Pike had described the few scattered towns as pleasing and hospitable. A few years later, pirates sacked coastal towns and armies of insurgents ran rampant over Texas, pillaging and burning. The Republican Army of the North cut a wide swath of destruction across Texas, damaging irreparably homes and public buildings at Nacogdoches, San Antonio, and Goliad. Only small, isolated El Paso escaped.

Spanish influence was still dominant in Texas' brief Mexican period in the first half of the nineteenth century. The plaza or town square, the fine arcades and patios of the more elaborate buildings and the tiny patios of humble dwellings, and the ambitiously developed plan of the haciendas were all retained as salient features of Spanish-American architecture in this period. Actually, however, very little building was done during the short Mexican rule, as the struggling

Mexican Republic was torn with strife at home and inadequately prepared to manage its over-extended frontier in Texas. Typical of Mexican construction was the small adobe hut with packed-earth floor and batten doors, and sometimes with loopholes cut for windows. Often these adobe houses were covered with plaster for beauty and for protection from weathering.

Mexico's chief contribution to Texas architecture lay in its Colonization Laws of the 1820's, which permitted empresarios to bring land-hungry colonists from the United States, Mexico, and Europe. Each of these groups carried its own architectural ideas to the wilderness of Texas.

The Anglo-Americans who came to Texas to build fortunes on the bounties of cheap land combined energy and resourcefulness in adapting the American type of frontier construction to the climate and available building materials of Texas. Being hard pressed for time to build dwellings for their families and to break land for their crops, the first settlers erected, Indian fashion, pole tents of hides or brush. The pioneers of Stephen F. Austin's first colony fashioned log shelters with three sides of logs, the south side being left open to the weather. As protection against driving rain and summer heat, the roof was often extended over the open side to make a porch. Then, as winter came, the settlers walled up the open sides of their cabins. A door and a window shutter, hung by hand-wrought hinges and easily barricaded from the inside, opened out under the porch roof. A stick-in-the-mud chimney completed a habitable log cabin.

The single log cabin later became the nucleus of the double log cabin. If an extended porch roof had been used, it became the roof of either a lean-to kitchen or a breezeway, or open hall, leading to another single room. This open hall between two rooms, which in the summer became a cool sitting room, was often called a dog-run or dog-trot.

During the period of Anglo-American colonization in Texas, the transition from dog-run log houses to frame structures was rapid. Clapboards were used to cover the substantial logs of the cabins. The dog-run was enclosed for a hall, and large chimneys were erected at the outside ends of the two rooms.

When money obtained from cotton brought affluence to ante-bellum Texas, the transformed dog-run house became a story-and-a-half home. In the 1850's, cotton boats plying the rivers of Texas often brought back fine fittings and furnishings from New Orleans. When a front gallery gaily ornamented with detailed grillwork was added to the old residence, the result was a typical Texas homestead.

There were many variations in these converted structures. One variant was the long house—in later times called the "shotgun" house, because a gun could be fired from the front door straight through every room to the back. The long house evolved from a single cabin by the extension of the roof over a new adjacent room on the end. As the family grew, additional rooms were added, each to the end of the one before.

Ranch-style houses also developed with the country. These wide, rectangular dwellings, one room deep, were covered with pitched roofs which often extended over the front and back porches. Since all the rooms afforded shaded cross-ventilation, the houses were very cool. The entire house was usually low on the ground, seldom more than one story high. Adobe or stone construction was frequently used, sometimes with a coating of stucco or whitewash. Long porches, some with decorative cornices, were common. Often there was a chimney at each end of the house. Inside, the fireplaces were of stone with plain mantels. The ceilings in many houses were covered with wide boards. These ranch-style houses, either of stone or of wood, were used all over Texas. Many examples are to be found in and around San Antonio.

The influence of the Old South is strongly felt in the architecture of the plantation homes of Texas. Some of the first Texas plantations were actually transplanted; the slaves, household effects, tools, building materials, and seeds were moved en masse from the South. These South-inspired plantation homes fall into two categories: the less pretentious houses, ranging from the single cabin to the semiclassical home, and the manorial dwellings of affluent and classical lines. Both the exteriors and the interiors of the smaller houses were usually built of wide boards. Their lines were simple and good, with sturdy chimneys and small front porches. The interiors were plain, with random-width flooring, lime-plastered or washed walls, board and batten ceilings, and millwork that ranged from crude to detailed.

Fate has been kinder to some of Texas' old manorial dwellings than to the more primitive structures. Many of them still remain, with their spacious, high-ceilinged rooms and cool wide double verandas or galleries supported by twin rows of pillars, as substantial evidence of the ease, grace, and hospitality of plantation life in the old days.

Another type of dwelling that has withstood the ravages of time is the rock house. Numbers of these structures, built of Texas stone and timber but often closely resembling the remote native homes of their builders, were erected in ante-bellum days along the Salado, Lampasas, and Little rivers. The houses of Castroville are representative of this transplanted architecture that made itself thoroughly at home in the Texas landscape. Solidly and honestly built, they have been whitewashed repeatedly for over a century, so that the sharp stone outlines have been almost erased and a delightful mellowness of texture and tint has been achieved. Slatted shutters can be closed into the window openings in the thick walls for protection from the sun. The comfortable dwellings are free of all clutter of unnecessary detail. Small houses were often built on the street, after the Alsatian-French fashion, leaving room in the rear for shady back yards and gardens full of flowers.

Bringing traditional forms of architecture with them in the 1840's, the German settlers at New Braunfels and Fredericksburg built in wood, mortar, and stone. Prince Carl zu Solms-Braunfels, founder of the German Immigration Society, wrote minute instructions for his colonists to follow in building their Texas homes, including

such directions as that houses be built well off the ground for protection against insects and that kitchen chimneys be fashioned of wood and stone in the shape of a pyramid. But these plans did not always work in the wilderness. John Meusebach, who took over the administration of the German colony, had the pioneers build first of logs and later of stone, using all native materials. The resulting houses were German in feeling, yet practical in the Texas environment.

A real innovation in Fredericksburg was the "Sunday house," of two rooms one above the other, with an outside stairway from the ground to the attic room, built for the convenience of country folk who came into town to church. The Germans also introduced half-timber and half-masonry construction; but they abandoned this form when they learned that the native stone would support itself. Woodcarving and handmade grillwork are more common in German houses than elsewhere. In the prosperous times before the Civil War, many German homes were built in a massive baronial style, some in the towns and others on large estates.

The colonial mansions of Texas, with their soaring two-story columns and gracious entrance halls, had their halcyon days in the later 1850's. In eastern Texas there are many fine examples of homes of the classical and Greek-Revival types.

French influence in ante-bellum Texas architecture may be seen both in imitation and in adaptation. Frequently the fine materials in homes that echoed those of France were brought by sea to Galveston, or by river to Jefferson, and carried by wagon train overland.

The adapted French architecture occasionally seen in East Texas came to this area from Louisiana. Cast-iron balcony rails and other ornamental features were imported from New Orleans. In the raised cottage the stair from the ground entered the second story, and the lower portion was on piers, usually bricked in. Characteristic of these cottages were the two porches, supported by brick or stone columns below and wooden ones above.

The influence of British and Irish architecture in Texas before the Civil War was negligible, although many settlers from the British Isles came to the region as planters and businessmen. Adaptations of Gothic and Tudor-Gothic styles are found more frequently in the churches than in the homes of this period. But some simple dwellings with thatched roofs do recall the modest homes of English rural areas; and craftsmen in the McMullen and McGloin Colony, which drew heavily from English and Irish stock, made use of some of the elements of their old-world homes in their houses and their homemade furnishings.

There are wide variations in the present condition of the ante-bellum homes still standing in Texas, and in the treatment that has been accorded them. Some of the old landmarks of the state are occupied and cherished by the descendants of their builders. In these homes may often be found furnishings and other relics handed down from the historic past. Other fine old structures are being used by commercial establishments for business purposes. These too may be well preserved and cared for, even though they may be remodeled inside to suit the needs of the occupants.

In the case of homes which had fallen into disrepair, restorations have been made—frequently quite faithful in their reflection of the qualities of pioneer dwellings. Some structures have been restored through private initiative and enterprise. Much worthy restoration work has also been done, in connection with the Texas Centennial in 1936 and at other times, by numerous civic and municipal organizations. Reproductions and reconstructions of old houses, such as those of the Twohig House and the Ruiz home on the Witte Museum grounds in San Antonio and the John Neely Bryan cabin in Dallas, may be found in many places in Texas.

Under the patronage of the Centennial Commission set up for the 1936 Centennial, markers have been set up commemorating sites, homes, historic shrines, and famous spots. The Daughters of the Republic of Texas, the Sons of the Republic of Texas, the Daughters of the American Revolution, and many civic organizations have acted as sponsors and custodians of the historic structures, relics, and ruins of Texas. Among the duties of the Texas State Historical Survey Committee established by Governor Allan Shivers is that of the restoration and preservation of historic homes and sites. And the Historic American Building Survey of the United States Department of the Interior has collected records of the present appearance and condition of a number of old homes judged by the advisory committee of the Survey to possess "exceptional historic or architectural interest" and has deposited them for permanent reference in the Library of Congress.

Unfortunately, however, many historic Texas homes have not been preserved. Floods and fire have destroyed venerable homesteads. Tenants have had little concern for the historical value of the houses in which they lived; absentee landlords have lost interest in upkeep. The march of progress is also responsible for the razing or radical remodeling of many old landmarks. In every large city historic homes have been dismantled to make room for modern skyscrapers, business houses, or civic establishments. In countless instances not even a marker has been placed to commemorate the site.

In spite of all this, however, there are left to the people of Texas many fine century-old homes to cherish and preserve for posterity. These mute relics of ante-bellum Texas have a living past, and they also have a promising future if the citizens of the state will continue to bestir themselves to preserve and maintain them as homes, shrines, or museums. The people of Texas should encourage and participate in movements to care for the state's landmarks, so that the varied patterns of building and living which entered into the formation of the Texas that now exists may never be forgotten.

Central Texas

The Spanish Governor's Palace

105 Military Plaza

ACCORDING TO THE DATE CARVED on the old keystone embedded above its front entrance, the Governor's Palace—now restored—was begun in 1749. Tradition places its first occupancy in 1756, when Governor Jacinto de Barrios took up his residence in the Palace on the Plaza de las Armas, which for many years thereafter was the center of all social and political life in the province of Texas.

But the two-century-old structure recalls many still earlier moments in Texas history. The story of San Antonio, with which the story of the Palace is interwoven, dates back to 1691, when Governor Domingo Teran de los Rios stopped while on an expedition across Texas at the Indian village of Yanaguana and gave the river on whose banks the village stood the name of San Antonio de Padua, because he had reached it on that saint's day.

In 1718, under orders from the King of Spain, Don Martin de Alarcon, Governor of Coahuila and Texas, founded on the San Antonio River the Villa de Bejar, named for the Duke de Bejar, who later became King Ferdinand VI of Spain. The Presidio, or fort, protecting the Villa was named San Antonio de Bexar, and the mission which Alarcon established was given the name of San Antonio de Valero, in honor of the Marques de Valero, who was then Viceroy of New Spain. The present Alamo was originally a chapel attached to this mission.

In 1729 King Philip V of Spain sought to strengthen Spanish rule over Texas by adding colonization to the mission-presidio system, which by itself had not proved satisfactory. In accordance with a plan developed by the Marques de Aguayo, Governor-General of Coahuila and Texas, settlers of a substantial character were brought to Texas from the Canary Islands. In 1731 fifteen families of Canary Islanders arrived in San Antonio after a long trek from Mexico. They settled on the west bank of the river, naming their new town the Villa de San Fernando. Given the privileges of *hidalgos,* noblemen, and land on which to settle, they organized the first complete city government in the province of Texas.

The first governor to rule over San Fernando was Captain Manuel de Sandoval, who was appointed in 1734. He made the Presidio of San Antonio de Bexar his official headquarters, coming there from the first capital of the province, Los Adaes, near the present site of Natchitoches, Louisiana. Sandoval's exact residence is not known.

Governor Barrios' occupancy of the Spanish Governor's Palace inaugurated a new era in the life of the capital. For decades all roads led to San Antonio, its Presidio, and the Villa. Well located and well fortified, the city served as headquarters for travelers into the wilds and offered them temporary protection. It survived when other Spanish colonies in Texas perished from want, neglect, or war. And its resident governor was the arbiter of fashion and manners. Priests versed in the classics, urbane officers of the regular army, and citizens of established lineage met at the Governor's Palace for dances and social functions. On the Plaza in front of the Palace the inhabitants from the chief magistrate down to humble townspeople joined in Mexican dances. Life in San Antonio was so pleasant that one governor, Don Antonio Cordero, established a precedent by deciding, upon retirement, to spend his declining years there.

But many flags were destined to fly over the Governor's Palace. The halcyon days ended when, in 1813, the Republican Army of the North ousted Governor Salcedo and took possession of the Palace and the town. Then San Fernando was retaken by the Spaniards, only to surrender again to the Mexicans in 1821. In 1835 Texas forces won possession of the priests' house, which commanded the main plaza. The fire they directed from that point forced General Cos to surrender,

The Spanish Governor's
Palace in San Antonio

Patio of Governor's
Palace

Doorway with keystone
bearing date 1749

but not before the Palace had suffered from the assault. Still further havoc was wrought in San Antonio when Santa Anna besieged the city and took the Alamo in 1836. After Santa Anna's later defeat at San Jacinto, the city in its new life under the Lone Star Flag of Texas began to grow away from the environs of the Governor's Palace.

In 1928 the city of San Antonio made plans to purchase and restore the old Palace, which had fallen into disuse and decay. Investigation into the title showed that the property belonged to the family of Gertrude Perez, a descendant of one of the Canary Island families. From the Perez family, which had owned it for over a century, the city bought the Palace in 1929 for $55,000. It had been used as a second-hand store, a restaurant, and a bar, which was known as "The Hole in the Wall."

After thorough research, the reconstruction of the old Palace was undertaken. Whatever remained was used; what had disappeared was duplicated as accurately as possible. Examples of such restoration may be found in the hand-hewn timbers, the wooden lintels, the wall brackets, and the wrought-iron lanterns. The four fireplaces in the building, all different, are all duplicates of the originals. In the *ante-sala* are San Antonio's first kiln-made tiles. The flagstone floors are partly originals. The unevenness of flagstones would have made dancing impossible, but in the days of the governors' *bailes* a layer of wax adobe on the ballroom floor made a smooth surface on which the dancers moved easily.

The long, low building is of adobe, covered with white plaster inside and out. There are ten rooms and a loft, reached by a winding staircase, where food was stored. At the right of the small entrance hall is the room of the Blessed Virgin, where the families of the governors worshiped. At the left is the *sala de justicia*, which was used both for the administration of justice and as a ballroom. The governor's office and several bedrooms are furnished in the traditional manner, with huge chests, large tables, and hand-carved beds. The dining room has a fireplace and a stone *lavabo* for washing the hands before eating. An open charcoal brazier heated the kitchen and provided for the heating of water and the baking of bread.

The elaborate patio has pebble-mosaic walks of intricate patterns winding through a garden of native shrubs and flowers and circling a central fountain.

The massive entrance doors of the Palace are carved with floral and symbolic ornaments. A popular legend points out that the history of the Spanish Conquistadores may be seen in the carvings if, reading clockwise from the top of the right-hand door, one interprets the seashells, dragons, infant face, flowers, cornucopia, Indian head, Conquistador's head, flowers, shields, dragons, medicine man's head, and final seashells to be seen in that order in the carvings as symbolic of the Conquistadores' journey, the dangers they encountered, the new land they discovered, its bounty, the Indians who lived in the land of flowers, the conquering of those Indians by force of arms, and the winning of the new land for the mother country across the sea.

The keystone above the doors contains, in addition to the date 1749, the Austrian coat of arms. King Philip V was an indirect descendant of Charles I, founder of the Spanish line of the Hapsburgs, member of the royal family of Austria-Hungary, and Emperor of the Holy Roman Empire. Knowing the Spanish line of Hapsburgs to have been extinct since 1700, Philip used the Hapsburg coat of arms when it suited his fancy. Thus it was that the two-headed eagle of the Hapsburgs was carved on the Palace of the Spanish Governor in Texas.

In March, 1931, the restored Governor's Palace was dedicated as a feature of the San Antonio Bi-Centennial celebrating the two-hundredth anniversary of the coming of the Canary Islanders who founded the Villa San Fernando. Since that year the Palace has been open to the public.

Open daily to visitors, except Christmas Day; Monday through Saturday, 9:00 a.m. to 5:30 p.m.; Sundays, 2:30 p.m. to 5:30 p.m. Admission fee: adults, 15 cents; children (7 to 14), 5 cents.

(*Above*) Central fountain in patio

(*Left*) Stone *lavabo* in dining room — for washing hands

(*Below, left*) Winding stairs from hallway to loft

(*Below, right*) Stove in kitchen used for heating and baking

La Villita

South Presa and Villita Streets

"RESTORED VILLITA," said the Villita Ordinance adopted by the City of San Antonio in 1939, will be a living example of indigenous Texan architecture, in itself an expression of our pioneer forefathers' reactions to the hardships and necessities of the times. Settled by the Spanish, "La Villita" was nevertheless on the far frontier and therefore original and independent in its conception.

At the time when the Villita Ordinance was adopted, under the administration of Mayor Maury Maverick, the area along the San Antonio River now enclosed by the stone walls of "Little Town" was junk-filled and squalid. But when the refuse had been cleared away, seven houses remained to be restored. Three, much older than the others, were of adobe, the rest of caliche—a soft, chalklike stone sawed from the banks of the river. The City of San Antonio, the National Youth Administration, and the Carnegie Foundation co-operated in the task of re-creating, on the old foundations of La Villita, a group of houses that should show the nature of the indigenous culture which had evolved there.

Because the original dates and owners of the houses of La Villita were not known, the restorations were to periods rather than to exact dates. From studies of other old San Antonio houses drawings were made to guide the restorers in supplying decoration, cabinetwork, hardware, etc. Mesquite doors and mantels were hand-carved by Mexican woodcarvers. An illustrative variety of window types and roof coverings were installed.

The history on which the restorers drew is a long one. When the San Antonio de Valero mission was founded in 1718, the soldiers who were to defend the mission were housed in La Villita in primitive adobe huts. The Canary Islanders who in 1731 settled in the Villa de San Fernando across the river looked down on the soldiers and their families. La Villita was on "the wrong side of the river" until 1819, when a flood which covered San Fernando left La Villita, on the high-est spot in the vicinity, dry. Then many of the more prominent people crossed the river to live, and La Villita became fashionable. The houses, still of stone and adobe, were enlarged and acquired patios and gardens.

A few Americans came into La Villita in the early 1800's—among them "Deaf" Smith, famous scout of the Texas Revolution; Captain Jack Hays of the Texas Rangers; and Sam Maverick and his wife Mary, who wrote what has become a famous account of the days when she was "San Antonio's first American woman." Then in the 1840's came a group of German settlers. Their contribution to the architecture of La Villita took the form of steep-pitched roofs and narrow porches, together with more and larger window openings. Some French, Alsatian, and Polish families followed. Finally, after the Civil War, La Villita became a quiet place which was gradually passed by in the progress of San Antonio, and which deteriorated steadily until its restoration in 1939.

Now, to the seven old houses two new ones have been added—one used for the preparation of food, the other a large two-story museum-library-forum-community building of squared stone patterned architecturally after the United States frontier military posts of the 1850's.

The buildings of restored La Villita house projects for the promotion of Latin-American culture and friendship. There are shops displaying weaving, ceramics, silversmithing, leathercraft, glass blowing, etc. The new "Little Town," with its flagstone walks and patios, its palms and native shrubs and vines in profusion, fulfils well the function assigned to it in the Villita Ordinance: to "enable this and succeeding generations to visualize in their true setting the significant events and personages in early Texan and American history of the Southwest."

Open daily to visitors, 8 a.m. to 6 p.m.

Restored La Villita or
"Little Town"

The San Martin House, one of the seven
restored homes in La Villita

A remnant of earliest San Antonio in the
shadow of a modern skyscraper

Cos House

513 Villita

ACROSS THE STREET from present-day La Villita, above the river and in an area which was part of the old Villita of San Antonio's earliest days, a long, low, plastered adobe house stands with its side to the street, facing on a secluded patio and presenting to the passer-by only a shuttered, ornamentally iron-barred street window. This structure is known as the Cos house, because General Martin Perfecto de Cos, brother-in-law of Santa Anna, lived in it for a time in 1835 and within its walls temporarily surrendered the Mexican forces to the Texas army.

When the first battles of the Texas Revolution were being fought in the fall of 1835, San Antonio became headquarters for the military force established over Texas-Coahuila by President Santa Anna. The Texas patriots under Stephen F. Austin marched against San Antonio, and for about a month they besieged the city. During the siege Austin was sent to Washington to ask aid of the United States for the new provisional Texas government, and command of the army outside San Antonio was turned over to General Edward Burleson.

The siege dragged on, and its abandonment was being considered when Colonel Ben Milam organized a force of some three hundred volunteers to attack the fort. By this time General Cos, who was commander of northern Mexico, had arrived from Matagorda Bay with about five hundred men and was defending the city. In the course of the battle which ensued, and which lasted from December 5 to December 9, Colonel Milam was killed. But his men won the battle, and on December 11 General Cos signed the articles of surrender to General Burleson, agreeing to return to Mexico with his entire force and never again to take up arms against Texas—a pledge which was broken the following spring at the Battle of the Alamo. On December 14, at dusk, General Cos led his vanquished troops from the Alamo and Villita areas of San Antonio.

The jubilant Texans immediately swarmed into the settlements, and the houses of La Villita were shuttered to protect their startled inmates from the noisy buckskin-clad soldiers.

The history of the Cos house, which reached its high point that winter day in 1835, dates back to the early 1800's. According to the abstract of title, the site was a grant, confirmed in 1797, to Don Antonio Martinez, who wished to enclose it as a corral for his cows. About 1812 his daughter, Maria Rafaela Martinez, took possession of the grant and made her permanent residence there. Again in 1830 the property was confirmed to her by the Jefe Politico of the Department of Bexar, with the approval of the Ayuntamiento (Council) of San Antonio.

Three months after General Cos left the house where he had surrendered to the Texans, the city was put under martial law by Santa Anna's armies. During these last days of Mexican supremacy in Texas, La Villita was once more occupied—and looted—by Mexican troops. Even in 1842, during the uncertain years of the Republic of Texas, General Adrian Woll and his Mexican army again struck at San Antonio and captured and briefly held the city. After those trying times the Cos house sank into oblivion like the other dwellings in La Villita.

But today the house has been restored and is maintained for community use. Its long main room has a beamed ceiling and a high corner fireplace. The double doors that lead to the shaded porch are louvered at the top, screening the view but admitting the breeze from the patio. Back of the house are grassy tiers of seats sloping down to the river, facing the small open-air theater on the other side which is known as the Arneson River Theatre, honoring E. P. Arneson, engineer in charge of the river beautification project which was begun in 1939.

Open daily to visitors, from 8 a.m. to 5 p.m.

The historic Cos house where General Cos temporarily surrendered the Mexican forces to the Texas army

Secluded patio of the Cos house

John Twohig House; Ruiz House

Brackenridge Park

THE JOHN TWOHIG HOUSE provides an excellent example of what can be done to preserve a historic landmark when the progress of a city overruns its original site. Built in 1841, the house stood for a full century on St. Mary's Street, at a location now commemorated by a marker placed by the De Zavala Chapter of the Daughters of Heroes of Texas. In 1941, when the growth of San Antonio made its removal necessary, the structure was carefully dismantled, with all its stones and its woodwork numbered and keyed to accurate blueprints, and assembled exactly as before on a spot on the grounds of the Witte Museum where the San Antonio River makes a bend much like the one on which the home was originally located.

The rear of the house, with its patio enclosed by a low stone wall, still overlooks the river. The novel outside stairway, which has a roof of its own, leads from the patio to the second floor. In this unusually planned house, the large parlor is on the upper floor adjacent to the bedroom, while the kitchen and dining room, on opposite sides of the entrance hall, occupy the ground floor.

The original owner of the substantial dwelling, John Twohig, was an Irish gentleman who became San Antonio's first big merchant, shipping goods to Mexico on a large scale, in prairie schooners. Among the patriots taken by General Woll in 1842 to the infamous prison of Perote in Mexico, he was one of those who managed to escape by digging through the prison walls. Back in San Antonio, Twohig abandoned merchandising and devoted his time to banking. Before his death in 1891 he accumulated a fortune of some three million dollars.

Many of the beautiful furnishings with which this prosperous merchant-banker equipped his home may still be seen there. In the dining room are large tables, a German cabinet, and an ornate sideboard holding an elaborate coffee urn. The bedroom contains, among other fine relics, a handsome four-poster bed and a capacious wardrobe. In the second-floor living room is a square piano which belonged to John Twohig's sister, Miss Kate Twohig, who presided over his household after his wife's death.

ALSO ON THE GROUNDS of the Witte Museum is the reconstructed home of the Texas patriots José Francisco Ruiz and his son, Francisco Antonio Ruiz. This very old house was originally built in 1745 on the Military Plaza. During the dedication ceremonies held in 1943 at the Witte Museum following the reconstruction of the house, Dr. Walter O. Stuck summed up its history:

The three generations of the Ruiz family who resided in the house saw the arrival of the first member from Spain, the prominent activities of the second generation in the development of Texas liberty, and finally the last descendant witnessed the union of Texas with the United States.

The Ruiz house is first mentioned in the will of Juan Manuel Ruiz, father of José Francisco, who died in 1797. It is referred to as "a stone house and a stone room adjoining on the corner of the Calle Real called de la Flores." It is again referred to in the Act of the Cabildo (town council) in 1803 when the residence was designated as the first schoolhouse in San Antonio and José Ruiz was named its first schoolmaster.

A typical ranch-style dwelling of the early days, the Ruiz house is built close to the ground, with a chimney at each end, evenly spaced doors and windows, and a roof extending over a low porch which runs the length of the building, providing an area of cool shade.

Both of these houses are open daily to visitors, except Mondays, from 10 a.m. to 5 p.m. Admission fee: 10 cents.

Patio at the rear of the Twohig house
overlooking the San Antonio River

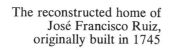

Home of John Twohig, an early
San Antonio merchant

The reconstructed home of
José Francisco Ruiz,
originally built in 1745

Lewis House 112 Lexington

"The Argyle" Corner of Patterson and Argyle

THE NAT LEWIS HOUSE, one of San Antonio's finest ante-bellum homes, was built by a New Englander for whom it was a final harbor after an adventurous early life of seafaring, shipwreck, and wandering. Found penniless at Port Lavaca, Texas, and befriended and brought to San Antonio by Don Galisto de la Garza, Nat Lewis became in time the owner of a store on the city's Main Plaza.

Lewis prospered mightily. In addition to building up great holdings in real estate in and around San Antonio, he became one of the cattle kings of Texas, with herds grazing from the Medina River to the Gulf.

The home Lewis built and in which he lived until his death in 1872 was in keeping with his Texas-made fortune. It is a two-story cut-stone mansion of enduring charm and hospitable mien. Its high ceilings, substantial chimneys, and double windows are characteristic features of Anglo-American architecture of ante-bellum days. The elaborate front doorway, sheltered by an ornate porch and decorated with side lights, gives the house a welcoming air.

When in 1921 a flood struck San Antonio, water rose almost to the second floor of the Lewis mansion, which stands only a few yards from the river bank. But the sturdy structure withstood the flood with little damage, as did the original smokehouse and slave quarters in the rear.

Although the Lewis house was once in the finest residence section of San Antonio, it is now surrounded by business and is itself occupied by a business concern. The original building remains intact, however, as do the separate structures behind it.

"THE ARGYLE," for years a fine country place on a land grant originally comprising 99,000 acres, is now enveloped in the city of San Antonio. The date of the building, although not known with certainty, is thought to be about 1850. It is placed definitely as an ante-bellum structure by the listing of its location as "Arsenal Lot No. 13," a designation arising from the fact that before the Civil War the government began construction of an arsenal near by.

Originally "The·Argyle" was a cross-shaped, two-story stone house. Its solid rock walls were some eighteen inches thick, and its floors and woodwork were made from stout cypress. The heavy timbers for the building were shipped from New Orleans and brought overland from the coast.

A third story was added some time before 1880. Evidence supporting this dating is found in the handmade nails used in this portion of the structure. A double front gallery was added, extending across the front of the house, with ornamental balustrades and finely proportioned pillars.

During its century of existence, the impressive dwelling became a rich storehouse of antiques. Some of the original silver, cutlery, and furniture remained in the house for many years, as did decorative pieces imported from foreign lands to stand in the large parlors and central hallways. Canopied beds and quaint chests created a colonial atmosphere in the bedrooms. The kitchen, with its beamed ceiling, was well equipped with iron pots and copper pans.

From 1893 until 1940, "The Argyle," then owned by the O'Grady family, was a hotel noted for its fine cuisine. Miss Lucy White, who owned the house from 1943 to 1955, deserves much credit for maintaining the old building. Recently the house was bought by the Southwest Foundation for Research and Education for use as a clubhouse for the Foundation's staff and board members.

Neither of these houses is open to visitors.

The cut stone mansion of Nat Lewis

Slave quarters, with smokehouse in the
foreground, of the Nat Lewis home

"The Argyle," for many years
a hotel noted for
its fine cuisine

Joseph Carle House and Store

Public Square

"DROPPING INTO CASTROVILLE," architect David R. Williams has written, "is finding peace. A weight is lifted from your soul; for here you are free from the strident discord of the multitudes of false forms and lines and colors that scream at you from almost any angle of our modern streets. Castroville is quiet." And he suggests that we may see in the little houses of this lovely old town a natural Texas art which Texans could use as the source of a beautiful architecture that could be called the state's own.

The origins of Castroville are Alsatian-French. Henry Castro, founder of the town, was a Frenchman and a member of Napoleon's honor guard. He came to America in 1827. Later, because of his efforts to negotiate a loan for the Republic of Texas, he was given a colonization grant and brought to Texas 485 families and 457 single men, most of them from Belgium and Alsace.

Castroville was settled in 1844. Only at great cost were the pioneers able to maintain the settlement. The first difficulties of clearing land and building homes were magnified by the constant threat of Indian attacks. Then came drought and famine. When the rains finally came and seeds once more began to sprout, a scourge of grasshoppers descended upon the crops and destroyed every green sprig. Then cholera broke out and men died even while burying the dead. When the epidemic at last subsided, the survivors praised God and immediately began plans for building a new church. This little stone building, constructed in 1847, is still standing on the campus of Moye Military School.

The first houses built in Castroville were hurriedly thrown up by men who expected nothing from their construction but shelter from the elements. Mrs. Julia Nott Waugh describes these first dwellings as

sometimes of stone, but more often . . . of logs, put together with pegs for lack of nails, and well chinked with grass. The dirt floors were so hard that good housewives not only swept but washed them; and the roofs, made of plaited grass or of the tules which grew abundantly in the river, were a satisfactory protection from sun and rain.

Gradually better houses were built as the settlers became established. Castro records in his diary a banquet for the "inauguration of my two houses, one built of briquets, the other of stone."

One of the largest of the Castroville structures, the Carle house and store, which was erected in the 1850's, stands fronting the wide public square at the north corner of Angelo and Madrid Streets. Although its architecture might be described as primarily French Provincial, its balcony, swung on wrought-iron brackets, is suggestive of Monterey.

The building is constructed of native limestone and cypress wood. The store, in the lower floor of the two-story front section, consists of a large room twenty-five by forty feet and a warehouse sixteen by thirty-seven feet, with a hall and a cellar beneath.

The one-story wing at the rear of the building and the second story above the store form the residence. The lower portion consists of a kitchen, pantry, dining room (with cellar below), and a porch which leads to an outdoor court and well. Over the store are a hall, a living room, and three bedrooms. Random-width flooring is used throughout, and the hall and one bedroom have wood ceilings. The handrail of the stairway is walnut, with an interesting six-and-a-half-inch carved newel.

Now occupied as a residence by Mrs. Sebastian Marty, the house is open to visitors only by appointment.

The Joseph Carle house
and store

Side view: living quarters
in wing at back

P. F. Pingenot House Lorenza and Petersburg Streets

Landmark Inn Florence Street

TYPICAL OF THE PLEASANT SMALL HOMES built by the settlers of Castroville once they had become well enough established to think not only of shelter but also of comfort and beauty is the Pingenot house. Built by an Alsatian, it may nevertheless, like its neighbors, be considered an example of indigenous Texas architecture.

The Pingenot house, plain and simple and without any needless decorative detail, is solidly and sturdily constructed. Its thick walls are of native rock, its woodwork and beams of mesquite and cypress and oak. The supporting beam in the roof is a mighty timber running in one piece the whole length of the house. The roof, pitched eight to twelve, was originally thatched; and while it is now of prosaic galvanized iron, one can readily imagine the charm its proportions must have given it in the soft-textured native materials of which it was first made. The walls, whitewashed many times, glow softly with the mellow tint of age.

The house consists of three large rooms, a small storeroom, and an open rear porch. It has a chimney at each end. Like many other Castroville homes, it is set very close to the street, leaving room at the rear for a private tree-shaded garden.

ANOTHER famous structure in Castroville may be seen across the highway at the opposite side of the village. For many years the Vance Hotel, it is now known as the Landmark Inn.

Soon after the founding of Castroville Caesar Monad, a French settler, built the lower floor of what is now the Inn, using it as a home and store. When John Vance purchased the property from Monad in 1853 he added a second story, using native stone and following the architectural style set by the original house. An outside stairway leads up within the high, cool two-story porch. Vance also built a home for himself near by, close to the Medina River, which today serves as an annex to the Inn.

For many years the Vance Hotel was an important stopping place for travelers to and from Mexico. Part of its renown came from its possession of a feature unusual in that time and place —a stone bathhouse, which added greatly to the comfort of travelers in the Texas climate.

Among the many famous travelers who stayed at the hotel was, it is said, Robert E. Lee, who stopped there on his way to Mexico, occupying Room 3. During the Civil War, when John Vance was postmaster of Castroville, the building also housed the post office. Even today the letter slots may be seen in the doors that face the street.

With the new century came new owners and varied uses for the old hotel. In the 1920's Jordan T. Lawler, a native of Louisiana, bought the house together with a mill and dam and supplied Castroville with its first electricity. Twenty years later, when World War II began, Ruth Lawler opened the place once more as Landmark Inn and housed many of the wives and relatives of cadets in training at near-by Hondo.

"Qui tient à sa tranquillité sait respecter celle des autres"—he who values his own tranquillity knows how to respect that of others—is the motto, like one from an old Alsatian hostelry, which hangs today in historic Landmark Inn, embodying the peace that surrounds the old houses of Castroville.

Miss Mary Balzer, owner of the Pingenot house, will show it by appointment. The Landmark Inn is open to visitors daily, 9 a.m. to 5 p.m.

Stone bathhouse,
an unusual feature of an
early Texas hotel

An Alsatian farmhouse built in Castroville by
P. F. Pingenot

Landmark Inn, an important stop for early-day
travelers to and from Mexico

Joseph H. Polley House: "White Hall"

North of Sutherland Springs

HIGH ON A KNOLL near Sutherland Springs, over-looking the Cibolo River and the rolling pastures that border it, stands "White Hall," the substantial stone house that was built in ante-bellum days by Colonel Joseph H. Polley.

The original Sutherland Springs, a few miles north of the present village through which Highway 87 passes southeast of San Antonio, is now a ghost town. Once, however, it was a resort where people from San Antonio spent their week ends, finding the journey from the city by horse and buggy not too long for comfort. Still to be seen beside the crumbling walls of the resort are the tall trees and the park area, which reportedly contains twenty-seven springs of hot and cold mineral water.

Attracted by the fertility of the soil of this area and the beauty of the banks of the Cibolo—a stream the Indians had given their name for buffalo—Colonel Polley purchased the land on the knoll from his son-in-law John James, and built his plantation home there. Polley had come from New York to Texas as one of the "three hundred" in Stephen F. Austin's colony, had married in 1821, and had settled near the Brazos at Bailey's Prairie, where he and his family lived until 1847.

The new home by the Cibolo was built solidly, with walls eighteen inches thick made of stones which were quarried near by. The supporting beams were of cypress wood, hauled great distances to the homesite. They were fastened together by wooden pegs. The woodwork for the house, turned in New York mills, made the long journey down the Atlantic Coast and across the Gulf to Indianola, thence by oxcart to the Cibolo. The ten rooms in the two-story house were warmed by five fireplaces. A log kitchen with a stone-chimneyed open fireplace stood behind the house, and an ingenious underground cistern which caught and held rain water was constructed in the yard near by.

Robert E. Lee, a close friend of the family, often stayed at the Polley home, joining in the social life of the family of eleven children. Frequently there were dances in the spacious hall of the mansion, for the long passageway in the center of the house lent itself well to these festivities.

Today white-faced cattle graze among the mesquite trees where once slaves cultivated the fields. But "White Hall" still stands as a notable example of an ante-bellum home soundly constructed and faithfully preserved.

(Above) "White Hall," farm home of Colonel Joseph H. Polley

(Left) Old log kitchen at rear of house

(Below) An ingenious water system leading to a large underground cistern

Two Erskine Houses

513 East Market and 902 North Austin

SEGUIN, FOUNDED ABOUT 1838, beautifully situated on the forest-lined Guadalupe River, and named for Colonel Josef Erasmo Seguin, leader of the only unit of Texas-born Mexicans in the Battle of San Jacinto, has one highly unusual distinguishing characteristic—many of its old homes are built, entirely or in part, of concrete. Dr. Richard Parks, a noted research chemist and one of the first to develop concrete for the construction of houses, came to Seguin about 1840 and settled there in 1842. The effect of his interest in that building material was so great that Seguin is sometimes called "The Concrete City." Frederick L. Olmsted, a traveler from the North who visited Seguin in 1855, wrote in *A Journey through Texas:*

A number of buildings in Seguin are made of concrete—thick walls of gravel and lime, raised a foot at a time, between boards, which hold the mass in place until it is solidified. As the materials are dug from the cellar, it is a very cheap mode of construction, is neat in appearance, and is said to be as durable, while protected by a good roof, as stone or brick.

Time has proved the visitor right about the durability of these concrete or part-concrete houses, many of which are still standing and in good condition.

Examples of homes which made use of concrete in combination with other materials are the two Erskine houses. The Erskine house on East Market, which was built sometime in the 1850's by S. N. Erskine, was originally a two-room log structure built around a ten-foot hallway. A porch which extended across the front was later enclosed to form lean-to rooms. These were at first covered with siding; but when A. M. Erskine purchased the property some years later, the siding was torn away and replaced by concrete. At this time, slave quarters and a kitchen, built of concrete by Dr. Parks, were also added. Panes of glass for the windows were brought by wagon from Port Lavaca. To this house was at one time attached the name "Hard Scrabble."

A HOME very different in appearance from this is the other Erskine house, more properly called the Humphrey home. The earliest portion of this house was erected in the middle 1850's at some distance from Seguin, by T. D. Spain. Around it a corral fence was built to pen in herds of cattle on their way to the Kansas markets. In 1867 the house was moved by Dr. D. H. Humphrey from the Prairie Lea district to its present location on North Austin; the corral fence was left intact.

The house is constructed of concrete and wood, the walls of the frame addition being filled between the studs with concrete. The original house was of only one story, with two rooms and a front porch. A double fireplace stood between the two rooms. The first addition was a room on the second story. Later four rooms were added, two on the first floor and two on the second, and the two porches were constructed, the upper gallery decorated by a balustrade. The house now has four fireplaces and a notable outside stairway leading from the lower to the upper porch. The entire framework of the house is mortised together, and the outside walls are of rough-sawn siding. Woodwork in the interior consists of cypress, yellow pine, and oak.

This lovely old home, with its feeling of comfort and grace, is typical of the better homes of the plantation type built in Texas in the 1850's.

These two homes are not open to visitors.

S. N. Erskine house, once known as
"Hard Scrabble"

Rear entrance of Erskine-Humphrey
house

Erskine-Humphrey
house

Zorn House: "Sebastopol" 704 Mill

J. D. Fennell House 202 East Walnut

THE STRIKING SQUARED-OFF TOP of the Zorn house contains evidence that Colonel Joshua Young, who built the house in the 1850's, was far ahead of his time; for the roof was so designed that a pool of water could be stored there to cool the house—a device now being used, in modified form, by contemporary hot-climate architects. In Colonel Young's day, the rooftop reservoir could also furnish a water supply in case an Indian attack should keep the family within the walls of the house.

"Sebastopol," as the home was named after the famous battle, was first occupied by Colonel Young's daughter, Mrs. Le Gette, whose granddaughter, Mrs. H. Y. McCallum, was the first woman to become Secretary of State in Texas. Later it was sold to Joseph Zorn, Sr., a Missourian by birth who came to Texas in 1840, married the granddaughter of Jeremiah Calvert, owner of the Magnolia Hotel in Seguin, and lived in Seguin all but ten of his eighty-three years, serving the town as mayor for more than twenty years and later as postmaster. It is still owned by a Zorn descendant.

The house is built of concrete in the shape of a T, with ground floor or basement rooms running along the cross of the T. An unusual stairway winds downward from the main floor, the last triangular tread ending directly below the top one. A secret passageway to the outside is said to be built into the walls.

The plan of "Sebastopol" is one often used in houses having ground floors. The main floor contained the living room, in this instance surrounded on three sides by a porch, and three bedrooms across the back. The ground floor was excavated only under the bedrooms, where the space was divided into kitchen, dining room, pantry, and storeroom. Flooring throughout the house is of five-inch pine boards. The dining room has a thirty-inch wood wainscot and a ceiling of the same beaded wood. The ceilings of the kitchen and storeroom are of painted canvas. The woodwork is walnut. All walls are plastered inside and out with limecrete of Dr. Parks's invention.

THE LOVELY Fennell house was built by W. C. Baxter in 1851, but has remained since 1860 in the hands of the Fennell family. Dr. J. D. Fennell, Sr., first of the Fennells to occupy the house, was the son of a Virginia family of French origin, but was himself born in Alabama. After studying in Baltimore and New Orleans he received his medical degree in Philadelphia in 1854. The next year he married and moved to Texas, settling in Seguin. During the Civil War he served as a surgeon in the medical corps of the Confederate Army of Virginia and saw active service at Bull Run. His son, Dr. J. D. Fennell, Jr., engaged in the general practice of medicine in Seguin and was a prominent member of the State Medical Association.

The Fennell home was originally a two-story house with four rooms around a central hall on each floor. Oak for floor joists was brought from Goliad and hand-hewn. The six to twelve pitched roof was first covered with hand-split cypress shingles. Oak and walnut made up the interior woodwork.

From time to time additions were made to the the house, one of them being the wing to the rear of the original section. Thus enlarged and modified, the house stands today beautiful in appearance and comfortable in arrangement, so well preserved that one might guess it to be a modern house, patterned after the ante-bellum homes of which it is actually a splendid example.

The Zorn house is open to visitors.

"Sebastopol," with rooftop
reservoir for water

J. D. Fennell's home, built in
1851 by W. C. Baxter

Side view of Fennell house

Parson Herron House Short Avenue and Mill

Hollamon House: "Elm Grove" 530 East Market

THE PARSON HERRON HOUSE is one ante-bellum Texas home which was not built of materials native to the region. Its hand-sawn stones, which were set solidly in place by Herron's slaves, are believed to have been brought across the Atlantic as ballast in a ship which made the return voyage from America to some European port with a cargo of cotton.

The two-story cellared stone house was built in the later 1850's by two brothers, Andrew and Alanson Herron. Andrew Herron, known as the "Fighting Parson," was a pioneer minister of the Presbyterian Church in Seguin. He deeded the home to Alanson and his wife, Ann.

The Civil War brought sorrow to the Herrons. Two sons were lost, one in the fighting at Gettysburg and one in a camp near Washington. After the war, Captain F. A. Vaughan bought the house. After retaining it for twelve years he sold it; but finding that he was unhappy elsewhere, he repurchased it in 1881. Part of the property he set aside as a family cemetery; and now the two who owned the house during those turbulent years, Captain Vaughan and Alanson Herron, rest there with their wives, Catherine and Ann.

The quarter-mile drive leading to the Herron home is lined with old mesquite trees, gnarled and bent, folding their slender foliage overhead. They provide a lovely welcome to a house which is itself remarkably beautiful in many ways. The mellowing effects of age and care may be seen in the satin-like surface of the black walnut used for the interior trim. There is a pleasingly proportioned mantel, and the wide-board window and door facings are admirably made. Another feature of the house is the fine stairway in the entrance hall. Its rail, of highly polished walnut, has delicately tapered spindles three-quarters the height of the average person mounting the stairs. In the rooms may be seen many choice pieces of period furniture that have been handed down to succeeding generations from the original owners.

THE HOLLAMON HOUSE, "Elm Grove," is closely tied to the Anglo-American beginnings of Seguin. French Smith, its builder, was the first president of the organization which was formed to lay out a plan for the town—on the lower half of the Branch league on the northeast side of the Guadalupe River, which had been purchased for the sum of three hundred pesos—and to sell lots. With the sale of each lot went the provisions that the property must be settled before the end of 1838, and that a substantial dwelling must be erected and lived in for one year.

Smith built his own home of oak logs, with four rooms around a center hall. When the Hollamon brothers, who were builders, arrived in Seguin from Virginia in the early 1850's and acquired the property, they soon contracted with Dr. Parks. To Smith's four rooms they added three rooms of Dr. Parks's concrete. For the interior they chose beautiful hardwoods of cypress, oak, and walnut. The long porch that now extends across the front of the house was also added at that time.

Two other houses built by the Hollamons still stand, one at 401 East Center across the street from the jail, the other on Mitchell Street in what is known as Guadalupe City (now within the city limits of Seguin). Both of these were built of Dr. Parks's concrete.

T. H. Hollamon was a lover of trees and refused to allow a single one to be cut from his property. Evidence of this is seen today in the long, winding drive that leads to the house, far back from the public street. Shaded and secluded, the old house retires behind the moss-draped branches that have towered over it so many years.

The Herron house may be visited in the afternoon by appointment; "Elm Grove" is not open to visitors.

The Parson Herron house, built of hand-sawn
stone blocks

"Elm Grove," home of T. H. Hollamon

Magnolia Hotel 203 South Crockett, Seguin

Andrew Ponton — Madden Fly House 424 St. Peters, Gonzales

LONG A STOP on the stage line, the older part of the Magnolia Hotel was constructed in 1840 from concrete of Dr. Parks's invention. Dr. W. S. Reid added the wooden portion in 1846. By 1849 the Jeremiah Calvert family owned and operated the hotel.

The foundation for the hotel is laid on one originally designed for a blockhouse planned in 1838 but never constructed because it was thought that the danger from Indian attacks was past. The Magnolia's builders must, however, have given some thought to possible danger of siege, for into the roof they built a water reservoir. When warnings of a raid were sounded on the Fourth of July, 1855, the citizens "forted up" in the Magnolia.

It was in the middle of the celebration that day that news came of marauding Indians who had killed two men and were on the warpath, headed toward Seguin. One of the Magnolia refugees later described the scene to her granddaughter, Miss Jennie Hollamon:

At the hotel the excitement was wild. . . . Upstairs the women were wringing their hands and weeping for safety of their husbands, who were to go out to meet the Indians, as well as for their own and their children's peril. Children were crying, and a perfect pandemonium reigned for a time. Pallets were placed all over the ballroom floor, but sleep was far away from the eyes of the restless women. A guard was placed at the Magnolia, while many men went out to meet "Wild Cat" and his braves. Once a search for Mrs. Reid (who owned the hotel) revealed her behind the dining room door sharpening her carving knives. "If it becomes necessary for me to defend myself," said she very earnestly, "I'd need a sharp knife."

At the northwest corner of the hotel there stood for many years an old stone block, on which a slave boy stood ringing his bell to signal the approach of the stage. Under the entire north side of the older part of the building is a cellar fifty by twenty feet cut from solid rock. Since it was the coolest spot in the hotel in the summer, it was used for storage. It is said that the walls of this cellar are honeycombed with holes which succeeding owners have dug in search of hidden treasure.

GONZALES, sometimes called the "Lexington of Texas" or the "Birthplace of Texas Independence" because it was the scene of the first battle of the Texas Revolution, is now a tranquil town of large oak-shaded homes, many of which date from ante-bellum days. One of these, a house so well preserved that it looks decades younger than its actual age, is the Andrew Ponton, or Madden Fly, home.

Ponton, alcalde of Gonzales, built the original cabin incorporated in the present structure in the latter part of 1837 or early in 1838. Later it was remodeled and used, during the Civil War, as a school. Still later Andrew Ponton's son, Tom, rebuilt the cabin and added half a story. In 1885 W. M. Fly purchased the house and converted it into a full two-story dwelling. In 1913 the columns were added when Warren Taylor, Fly's son-in-law, occupied the home jointly with him.

The remains of the chimney which the Pontons built are still intact, and under the present music room is the cistern. The ceilings in all the rooms are twelve feet high. The woodwork is hand made. The building material used in the original house was Pensacola pine from Florida, conveyed from the old port of Indianola by ox team.

The commodious porches extend not only across the front of the house, but also to the side. Some of the windows reach to the floor. Five upper and lower columns and an upper gallery railing lend an air of distinction and dignity to this home which has seen more than a century of change.

Neither of these houses is open to visitors.

Magnolia Hotel, built of concrete in 1846

The Andrew Ponton–Madden Fly house

Dr. Theodore Koester House

421 South Seguin

THE DR. THEODORE KOESTER HOUSE recalls the earliest and hardest days of New Braunfels; for Dr. Koester, as official physician of the Society for the Protection of German Immigrants in Texas, which under the leadership of Prince Carl zu Solms-Braunfels established the colony, came to the townsite on the Comal Springs with the first settlers in 1845. The next year he accompanied the second group of colonists on their terrible, fever-ridden march from Indianola to the new town which had been named for Prince Carl's estate on the Lahn River in Germany. He suffered with his people during that dreadful summer, when four hundred died of fever and dysentery.

The German settlers of New Braunfels did not, however, permit hardship and sickness to discourage them. When Ferdinand Roemer, the German geologist whom the Berlin Academy of Sciences sent to Texas in 1845, visited New Braunfels in 1846-47, he found the colonists building busily. Some of the houses, he reported, were of logs, some of studding framework filled in with brick; some were frame, and some were mere huts of cedar posts driven into the ground and roofed only with a tent canvas or with ox-hides. Most of the houses, he added, followed for coolness the American style of roofed-in porches. At the time of his arrival there were, he estimated, some eighty to a hundred such houses and huts in the colony. As he entered the principal street, Roemer related,

a small house attracted my attention upon which three shingles were hung, containing inscriptions, "Apothecary," "Dr. Koester," and "Bakery." . . . I at first concluded the "Baker" was a boarder, but my companion informed me that Dr. Koester actually united in his person the professions of apothecary, baker, and physician. . . . This combination must have been a fortunate as well as a lucrative one, for during my stay in New Braunfels, a new, neat, and roomy house rose near the old one in which the doctor and his young wife, whom he had chosen from among the immigrants, established themselves snugly.

The Koester house which is standing today was built later, in 1859 and 1860, from the plans of W. A. Thielepape, the local architect who also supervised the building of the first Comal County courthouse. The two-story home, built over a full basement, was constructed of native limestone. The walls of the basement and the first floor were made about eighteen inches thick.

Each floor, including the basement, was divided into five rooms. Originally, the basement contained the kitchen, pantry, and storage rooms. The first floor contained the dining room, which had china closets and cabinets with adjustable shelves, and to which food was carried by a dumb-waiter from the kitchen below. Also on this floor were a hall, a large living room, and the doctor's office.

The second floor consisted of three bedrooms, a hall, and a maid's room which was later converted into a bathroom. Between the largest bedroom and one of the smaller ones were folding doors, which were often used to advantage in the staging of home-talent plays, when the audience sat in the larger room and the smaller served as stage.

The stairways are noteworthy. A winding, fan-type stair affords easy climbing to the second floor. On the half-way landing of the cleverly constructed stairway to the basement is a door leading to the outside, so that only the lower half of the stairway need be used in the delivery of groceries and supplies to the basement.

Speaking tubes, antedating the modern telephone, connect the three floors of the old home, and other early features are still in use. Additions and improvements include the two bathrooms and a large glassed-in porch which now extends across the rear of the house.

Open to visitors by appointment.

Dr. Theodore Koester's home, built of native limestone

Ferdinand Lindheimer House 489 Comal

J. L. Forke House Seguin and Jahn

OF ONE HOUSE HE SAW on his visit to New Braunfels in 1846 Ferdinand Roemer wrote:

At the end of town, some distance from the last house, half hidden beneath a group of elm and oak trees, stood a hut or little house close to the banks of the Comal. It furnished an idyllic picture with its enclosed garden and general arrangement and position.

Before the door a black-bearded man was splitting wood. This was Ferdinand Jakob Lindheimer, the botanist, of Frankfort-on-the-Main, who had come to New Braunfels with the first settlers, collecting botanical specimens on the way up the Guadalupe River to the townsite.

Lindheimer, who had received in Germany a good schooling in mathematics and the classical languages, had at the same time conceived an ardent interest in botany. He had also become involved in politics, having taught in the Bunsen School at Frankfort for seven years, during which time six of the school's teachers had been sentenced for sedition. Like many other Germans then seeking to escape from government oppression, he had decided to go to America. He went to Texas in 1836, upon his return from a voyage to Mexico, to join the fight for Texas independence. When a brief trial of farming in 1840-42 showed him that he was not suited for that occupation, he made an arrangement with the botanists Asa Gray and George Engelmann to provide sets of Texas plants which were to be named and mounted by the two botanists and sold, so that Lindheimer might turn his lifelong interest in botany into a means of earning a livelihood.

During his collecting trips through the Texas wilderness, made with a two-wheeled, horse-drawn covered cart, Lindheimer would sometimes go for months at a time without seeing a human being. But after he had built his house in New Braunfels he made that town his headquarters; and in 1852 he closed his career as a botanical collector to become editor of the newly founded *Neu-Braunfelser Zeitung,* which he then managed for twenty years.

The land which was originally granted to Lindheimer as a colonist was designated in the map of New Braunfels as the "Botanical Garden." But today nothing remains of the garden, for the grant was divided into lots and sold by Lindheimer's heirs. The lot on which his home stands is the only part of the property now in the hands of the family. Before the simple white cottage is a Centennial marker naming Ferdinand Lindheimer the "Father of Texas Botany."

WE ARE TOLD that J. L. Forke, pioneer merchant of New Braunfels, was popular among the thrifty mothers of the young colony for always listing the lowest prices on Fleischer's knitted worsteds. The town was fortunate in having this enterprising merchant to provide a variety of goods in the midst of the wilderness. But life was not easy for the Forke family at first; the only way in which they could make a living when they first arrived from Germany was to work the field of the orphans' farm on shares—making thirty-two bushels of corn, which was immediately ground into meal for mush and corn bread.

But the town of New Braunfels grew, centering around the main street, Seguin. And here, on the corner of Seguin and Jahn, Forke built his log store and his home. The recorded deed shows that originally one Bracht purchased the lot in 1848 from the German Immigration Company for the sum of $60.00. The store, which stood lengthwise with Seguin Street and later was moved to the rear of the lot, is no longer standing. But the home, considerably remodeled, remains as a reminder of the early days.

Neither house is open to visitors.

Home of Ferdinand Lindheimer,
"Father of Texas Botany"

The J. L. Forke house

Major Edward Burleson House 2½ miles northwest of San Marcos

Arnold - Hefley House West Main, Cameron

THE MAJOR EDWARD BURLESON house near San Marcos was built by the son of General Edward Burleson, famous Indian fighter, general in the Texas army at San Jacinto, member of the Texas Congress, and Vice-President of the Republic of Texas. The original dwelling built by the elder Burleson in 1848 was a two-room cabin of elm and oak logs, floored with pine and roofed with rough hand-rived clapboards, with a rock chimney at the north end. After the Burleson family left the cabin it was occupied from time to time until 1910, when it was abandoned as uninhabitable. On June 30, 1932, the Moon-McGehee Chapter of the Daughters of the Republic of Texas erected at the site of the ruined cabin at the head of the San Marcos River a gray granite monument supported by stones from the original fireplace.

Edward Burleson, Jr., eldest son of General Burleson, who was born in Tennessee in 1824 and came to Texas with his parents in 1831, spent the early years of his life in the family home. Like his father, he distinguished himself in military service—in the Mexican War, with the Texas Rangers, and in the Civil War—winning the rank of major.

The large two-story rock and brick house which Major Burleson built as his family's new home stands on the farm he owned a few miles northwest of San Marcos. It was the birthplace of Albert Sidney Burleson, who became Postmaster General in President Wilson's Cabinet.

The house, which has been perfectly preserved by the Knispel family for almost forty years, is roomy, with an ell running to the rear on one side. The walls and partitions are eighteen inches thick. The two rooms on either side of the large entrance hall are spacious. Behind these three "front" rooms are three smaller ones. The kitchen and other utility rooms form the rear wing. An outside stairway leads from the lower veranda to the second-story gallery, which is surrounded by an ornamental railing. The house, set in surroundings of great beauty, is flanked by mighty oaks draped with gray Spanish moss. Mrs. Lena Knispel, widow of A. F. Knispel, is the present owner and occupant.

STANDING in the heart of the business district of Cameron, the county seat of Milam County, is the beautiful, rambling one-story home of Captain B. I. Arnold. The builder of the log cabin which formed the nucleus of this house, as similar cabins did of so many others, was John A. Buckholts, a lawyer who came to Cameron in 1852. A few years later he added the frame construction, using planks sawed by the small sawmill which was in operation at Cameron at that time, from wood obtained in the Little River bottomlands. It is said that the planks are held together with old blacksmith nails. The ceilings in many of the rooms are of ten-inch boarding.

In 1878 Captain and Mrs. B. I. Arnold purchased the property, and through the years they made additions to the house. At present many wings and ells extend from the main portion of the structure—one ell boasting a decorated cornice of much charm. The modern look of the house with its white siding and green shutter trim belies its actual age. The entrance porch, suggestive of the Greek Revival period, lends an inviting atmosphere which is intensified by the double doors with their side lights. In the grounds, surrounded by a white picket fence, old trees and shrubs are supplemented by modern plantings.

Until her recent death Mrs. Mamie Arnold Hefley, daughter of Captain and Mrs. Arnold and a leader in educational and cultural circles in her community, maintained the old family home with great care and affection.

The Burleson house is open to visitors on Sunday afternoons by appointment.

Major Edward Burleson's home

The Arnold-Hefley house

Peter Tatsch House

210 North Bowie

THE PETER TATSCH HOUSE is one of the finest examples of the old stone houses of Fredericksburg, which in their simplicity, sturdiness, and craftsmanlike use of native materials are among the most beautiful of all early Texas homes.

Remembering the German villages along the Rhine, the pioneers of Fredericksburg laid out their town in the Texas hills around one long street. Their first crude houses of post-oak logs set upright in the ground were soon replaced by houses of the German *Fachhaus* type, built of upright timbers with the spaces between filled with rocks and plaster. When the builders found that the stone quarried near Fredericksburg could support its own weight, they began to construct thick-walled limestone dwellings, many of which, mellowed to an amber color by the sun and rain of nearly a century, stand today as solidly as in their earliest years.

Peter Tatsch built his stone house in 1857. A German burgher, he migrated to Texas with a company of German colonists under the leadership of the visionary Prince Carl zu Solms-Braunfels and later of his more able successor, John O. Meusebach. The Tatsch home is a masterpiece of workmanship. Because of the scarcity of tools, most of the rocks were picked to fit or chipped to a line. Few of them show any sign of dressing except by a hammer; yet all the stones fit perfectly. They are neatly held in place by a lime mixture which was made in a kiln standing on the east bank of Town Creek, a few blocks from the post office.

The house contains two large rooms and a side room running the entire length of the building. A fireplace of ordinary size heats one of the large rooms. The house walls are about fourteen inches thick. The inside walls and ceilings of the two large rooms are plastered and painted white, and the framework of the simple door and the several windows is also white. Built into the living room wall is a recessed closet, which was used as a medicine chest and storage vault for valuable papers. Its highly polished wooden door was handmade and expertly fitted.

But the most striking thing about the Tatsch house is the enormous Dutch chimney which is attached to the side room, or kitchen, extending some nine feet across the entire east side of the room. The fireplace is large enough to accommodate whole logs of cordwood, uncut. An iron rod running its entire width still holds iron hooks and chains which were once used to hang kettles and other utensils. In the early days, the fireplace heated the kitchen and the family meals were cooked in it. It was also used for the making of syrup and the curing of large quantities of meat, not only for the Tatsch family but for the entire community. Dutch ovens are still used to bake bread on its hearth. The chimney was specially constructed to carry away all soot and smoke and to regulate the draft.

After his house was finished, Peter Tatsch himself made the furniture, most of which remains today. In the two main rooms are two bedsteads of native hackberry and black walnut. In the living room stands a wardrobe some six feet high, four feet wide, and two feet deep, a masterpiece of cabinetwork, made of native cherry from trees felled in the vicinity of Fredericksburg.

For many years this home, which exemplifies the success with which the German colonists adapted the ideas they had brought from their fatherland to the materials and surroundings of a stark frontier, was occupied by Peter Tatsch's descendants. The present owner, Walter Tatsch, is a grandson of the builder.

This house is not open to visitors except by special arrangement.

The sturdy stone house of Peter Tatsch

Enormous Dutch chimney attached to the kitchen of Tatsch house

Kiehne-Foerster House; Nimitz House and Hotel

Main Street

THE KIEHNE-FOERSTER HOUSE, built of stone and timber in 1851, is reputed to have been the first two-story house in Fredericksburg. All the wood of the hand-hewn native timbers is expertly cut and shaped. Windows with circular heads and heavy double doors are recessed deeply into the thick walls. The house has upper and lower porches, decorated by railings and connected by an outside stairway.

William Kiehne, the builder and first owner of this house—which stands today on Main Street in an excellent state of preservation—was a friendly soul. Though he lived in town, he was an intimate friend of Berg, the old Hermit of the Hills in Gillespie County. Kiehne often wandered into the hills to watch the hermit crush his own corn with his improvised mill or play on his handmade pipe organ. When Kiehne bought a large tract of land that included the hermit's hut, he not only did not dispossess the recluse, but gave him life tenure in his solitary dwelling.

THE OLD NIMITZ HOUSE is of the type of steep-roofed, limestone-walled houses that rest behind their railed porches close by the walks on either side of the wide main street of Fredericksburg. Following the style of the German *Fachhaus,* these homes were often built, as was the Nimitz house, with outside stairways as entrances to spacious attics.

Born in Germany in 1826, young Charles H. Nimitz came to America in the 1840's as a sea captain. In 1846 he journeyed from South Carolina to Fredericksburg as one of the town's first colonists. That same year he built the first section of the Nimitz Hotel, a one-story frame structure. Some years later he added another one-story section, this time of stone, which was used as a saloon. Still later he built the famous "Steamboat" portion of the hotel, formed in the shape of a ship with the prow extending out into the street.

In 1861 Charles Nimitz gained the title of "Captain" on land rather than at sea, when he raised the Gillespie County Rifles for the Confederacy. He was made enrolling officer of the frontier district, in which post he remained until the end of the war. Ammunition for the guns and pistols of his men was secured at Fredericksburg's gun cap factory. Captain Krauskopf, a gunsmith, and Adolph Lungkwitz, a silversmith, combined their skills to make a machine for rolling copper and cutting caps. For the loading and priming of the caps they got saltpeter from bat caves in the hills near Fredericksburg and imported quicksilver from Galveston. Krauskopf also made guns of different patterns and calibers; and his guns and caps were used not only in the Civil War, but also during Texas Indian troubles.

Military heroes were among the celebrities who stayed at the Nimitz Hotel during the early years. One of the many antiques still in use at the hotel is the spool bed on which General Robert E. Lee slept on his frequent trips to old Fort Marion Scott, near Fredericksburg, while he was stationed at Fort Mason for some months before the Civil War.

Captain Nimitz took part in civic and state affairs, as school trustee while his eight children were growing up, as vice-president of the Gillespie County Fair, the oldest fair of its kind in Texas, and as a member of the state legislature. He managed the hotel until his death in 1911, when his son, C. H. Nimitz, assumed control. The name of Nimitz, associated both with the hotel and with the simple white cottage on Main Street, is an honored one in Texas, made illustrious most recently by Admiral Chester A. Nimitz, who was born in Fredericksburg.

The Nimitz house is not open to visitors.

Captain Charles Nimitz'
home, in the style of
the German *Fachhaus*

The old Nimitz hotel
before it was rebuilt into
a modern structure

The Kiehne-Foerster house,
built in 1851

Sunday Houses; Staudt Sunday House

223 West Creek

NOT ALL THE GERMAN SETTLERS of the Fredericksburg area lived in town. Many of the prosperous farmers and ranchers had their homes among the rolling hills, too far away to share in the daily benefits of shops and churches in the community. But the ingenuity of the settlers provided a way in which they might keep up with the townspeople on Main Street. Many of the farmers who lived within a radius of twenty miles from Fredericksburg bought town lots and built "Sunday houses," small and inexpensive but substantial and comfortable, to shelter their families in town over the week end. Thus they started a custom, still prevalent, which permitted them to be near their friends and relatives while attending church or social affairs or doing the weekly shopping, without imposing on anyone.

Gillespie County is probably the only area in the United States where Sunday houses were built for this purpose. Though there were a few such houses in Harper and other small towns in the county, the idea originated in Fredericksburg, where dozens of the miniature houses were erected. Several of them are still standing.

Sunday houses were usually built of stone, although sometimes timber was used by builders who had wooded tracts. Some were one-story dwellings of two rooms; but the most interesting type had the two rooms one above the other, with a space-saving outside stairway connecting the two. These small houses were furnished for light housekeeping, with a fireplace to heat at least one of the rooms and to serve as a place for preparing meals.

THE STAUDT HOUSE, before it was remodeled and enlarged by Karl Henke, constituted a typical Sunday house, and many of the characteristic features of these houses may still be seen in it. While the outside stairway has been removed, traces of its attachment to the stone wall are still visible, as is the little door behind the chimney by which entrance was gained to the upper room. The original grant for the property on which this house is located was made by the German Emigration Society to George Geyer in 1847. Geyer, a bachelor, built the small house of native stone and timber. A story is current that he was shot and killed as he stood in his own doorway, by outlaws hiding behind the large oak tree in front of the house. This house, which has changed owners several times, was owned for many years by Christian Staudt.

For the convenience of out-of-town members who had no Sunday houses, several Protestant churches of Fredericksburg provided small buildings on the church grounds which were equipped with stoves, cooking utensils, benches, and tables. Here churchgoers who lived in the country could prepare their lunches. But for overnight stays the Sunday houses were ideal—nor were they used on week ends alone. Frequently a farmer or rancher who wished to send his children to school in town would use his Sunday house while school was in session. And occasionally an aging farmer turned his farm over to his son, built another room and front porch on his Sunday house, and retired to the "city."

The Staudt Sunday House is open to visitors daily from 1 p.m. to 5 p.m.

One of Fredericksburg's "Sunday Houses"

The Christian Staudt home, once a
"Sunday House"

Side view showing traces of the
outside stairs attachment and
upper entrance door near chimney

Crocheron House 300 Block Wilson

Wilbarger House Main Street

BASTROP, THE TOWN named for Felipe Enrique Neri, Baron de Bastrop, through whom Stephen F. Austin secured his first grant for colonization from the Spanish government in 1821, failed to make much of an impression on at least one traveler who visited it in the 1840's and afterward wrote:

About 80 or 90 frame houses, painted white, stood on several broad, straight, unpaved streets. Among them were 6 or 8 stores and 3 or 4 saloons. Most of the houses looked rather dilapidated, and the place needed a "new start" apparently to keep it from losing its appearance of a town altogether.

But by 1857, when Henry Crocheron arrived in Bastrop, the town had made the needed "new start." And Crocheron himself did much to help it along by building, for himself and the wife he married not long after settling in the town, a fine home in the classical style. Crocheron, who was of Dutch descent and came to Texas from Staten Island, New York, prospered greatly as a pioneer Bastrop merchant. His house, constructed almost entirely of cedar which was cut and milled on the owner's property and finished by hand, is an imposing two-story structure with a fine double portico crowned by a beautifully proportioned and nicely detailed wood entablature.

The interior of the house is different in arrangement from most of those planned during this period in Texas in that the entrance hall runs the width, rather than the length, of the house. This plan sets the stairs, with their lovely hand-carved walnut rail and newel, to the left of the entrance door instead of directly in front of it. From the reception hall one could go to the left into the music room, with the cistern room and kitchen behind, or to the right into the parlor, behind which was the dining room, decorated with a three-foot wood-paneled wainscot. Upstairs were two bedrooms and a sewing room. The house is said to have been the first in this locality to have windows "with weights."

JOSIAH PUGH WILBARGER, Bastrop colonist who settled on his league of land at Wilbarger's Bend, is perhaps best remembered for having lived through a scalping by Indians. The gruesome episode occurred when Wilbarger and a neighbor named Hornsby, with some other friends, started out on horseback for an exploring trip. While they were eating lunch beside a spring, the Indians surrounded them and fired upon them. In the fight that followed Wilbarger was felled by an arrow in the leg and a bullet in the neck. The Indians, supposing him to be dead, scalped him and took his clothing. Wilbarger later described the scalping as the sound of accumulated roars of thunder. Though he lived for eleven years after this terrible experience, his death was in part caused by the scalping, for he died after striking the sensitive spot on his head on a low doorframe in his gin house.

Today the Wilbarger home, like many other old houses in Bastrop, stands in a splendid state of preservation. It is a typical two-story frame house with a central hallway flanked by side rooms and anchored with sturdy chimneys. Lower and upper porches have double sets of columns, and the windows are shuttered.

During its full century of existence, the house has been used as residence for four generations of the Wilbarger family. Many antiques and relics of the early days still have their place in the old dwelling, which is currently occupied by a great-granddaughter of the original owner. On the walls are to be seen a copy of Josiah Pugh Wilbarger's application to the Mexican government for admittance to Texas and a request for a league of land in Austin's colony written in 1832, together with a citation by the Historic American Buildings Survey of the United States Department of the Interior, placed in 1934.

The Wilbarger house is open to visitors; the Crocheron house is not.

Residence of four generations
of the Wilbarger family

Henry Crocheron's home,
built almost entirely of cedar

Stagecoach Inn: "Shady Villa"

Highway 81

BESIDE SALADO SPRINGS and on the site of an old Tonkawa Indian village is the famous stagecoach relay station and inn which, because of the magnificence of its trees, was long known as "Shady Villa." In the earliest days, the Inn stood at the crossroads of the Chisholm Trail and the Old Military Road marked by Colonel William Cooke in 1840—an important highway of its time, connecting a chain of forts from the Red River to the Rio Grande. Later, with the influx of pioneers and colonists, the Overland Stage Line chose the road as its route from Little Rock to San Antonio. The Inn then became a stop and relay station for the Overland stages—the most colorful era of the old building's history, and the one which gave it its present title of Stagecoach Inn. In those days,

. . . the arrival of the stage with a rattle and a clatter and a tooting of the driver's horn was a very thrilling event at the Inn where everybody rushed to the veranda to greet the passengers and pick up the mail —about four months old—while the horses were changed at the relay barn in the rear.

Sam Houston, Stephen F. Austin, and James Bowie were among the many illustrious Texans who stopped at the Inn during the early years. Later there were others such as Robert E. Lee. But not all were men of the same sort of fame. Close to the Inn is the entrance to a cave containing a flowing spring, the water from which is now piped to the building. In the wilder days of Texas the cave, with its supply of good water, is reputed to have been used as a refuge by Sam Bass and others who did not want their presence too widely known. The cave is said to have been furnished at one time with sleeping facilities for these exceptional guests.

Much of the Inn's patronage, however, was of an entirely different sort. The hostelry even contributed to the progress of higher education in Texas. In 1860 Salado College was built on College Hill, across the road from the Inn, which sheltered and fed many of the students of that noted pioneer institution.

As the number of travelers seeking its hospitality increased, the Inn grew. First a second story was added to the original two rooms. Later the available accommodations were doubled by the addition of an extension on the north.

When the great days of its prominence as a stage stop had passed, the structure gradually deteriorated. But today, thanks to Dion Van Bibber, who when he purchased the property had the vision to undertake restoration in the spirit of the original Inn, the atmosphere of the early days has been renewed along with the physical makeup of the building. Constructed of wide pine planks, the Inn has limestone fireplaces in both downstairs and upstairs rooms. When a fireplace was restored, the original base was left intact, the new portion simply being added to the old. Whenever a change was necessary, every effort was made to utilize materials already part of the building. Flooring from the second story, for example, furnished wide boards for the attractive dado in the downstairs area which is now the tearoom. The original railless stairway remains untouched.

The result of this skilful work is a hospitable place where the hungry traveler may, as he steps over the threshold from the rush of traffic on a modern highway, feel that he is actually entering an inn of ante-bellum Texas.

Hospitable Stagecoach Inn, once an important relay station on an overland stage route

Side view of "Shady Villa"

Colonel E. Sterling C. Robertson House

Southwest of Salado

LESS THAN A MILE southwest of Salado is the twenty-two-room, hundred-year-old home of Colonel Elijah Sterling Clack Robertson, son of an early Texas empresario. One of the few original homes built on a colonial grant still standing to this day, the Robertson house has been lived in continuously by the same family for an entire century. It is perhaps unique in Texas today in that it represents the complete plantation unit with house, grounds, slave quarters, stables, and burial grounds.

The plan of the house includes three parts—the main two-story unit, a kitchen-dining-service unit, and the original stone slave quarters. Both the upper and lower floors of the main section have front gallery rooms. On the first floor, these serve as guest rooms. By architectural duplication the "wayfarer's room" and the storage room in the rear maintain the planned symmetry of the building. The storage room, perhaps the most important room of all in a plantation house, is equipped with two immense closets and built-in cabinets. In addition to these rooms the lower floor contains a central reception hall, master bedroom, rear sitting room, parlor, and library. The colonial stair in the reception hall is made in its entirety—treads, risers, wall stringer, balusters, newel, and handrail—of dark mahogany. The octagonal spindles are pegged into the railing and dovetailed into the treads.

The upper story of the main building is an exact duplicate of the lower one in plan, with space provided for seven bedrooms. The complete plan of the house, which was built in 1856-60, includes not only the twenty-two rooms but also two stairways, two halls, four porches, and eleven fireplaces.

The kitchen-dining-service unit, which is constructed of native limestone, comprises five rooms—a dining room, a kitchen, a produce room, a laundry, and a meat room. Immediately back of the large dining room, with its wall cupboard and

stone mantel, is the kitchen, which is provided with an ample fireplace. The service rooms adjoining the kitchen show exposed rafters overhead. The laundry room, which has a cistern, and the dirt-floored meat room complete the unit.

The stone slave quarters, an interesting feature of ante-bellum houses now rarely found intact, are made up of six rooms. All lintels and sills are limestone, as are the walls. There are three double fireplaces, so arranged that each room has an opening. A door leads from each room directly to the outside.

The chapter of Texas history with which this house is associated is a most interesting one. The father of the builder, Sterling C. Robertson, was an empresario—that is, an agent who was granted a contract by the Mexican government for the introduction of families to establish colonies in Texas. The empresario system greatly speeded the colonization of Texas between 1821, when the first such grant was made—originally by Spain to Moses Austin, then by Mexico to his son Stephen F. Austin—and 1836, when the need for it was ended by the Texas Revolution. An empresario not only arranged for the settlement of his colonists, but had wide authority over them in economic, military, and judicial matters.

Before coming to Texas Sterling C. Robertson had served in the United States Army against the Indians and the British. In 1823 he toured Texas and became interested in the country. In 1825 Robert Leftwich, as empresario, obtained a grant from the Mexican government to settle families north of the Old San Antonio Road. Somewhat later these rights were transferred to Robertson, who had formed the Nashville Company for colonization. In 1830 part of the company's contract for two hundred families was still unfilled; and the next year the grant was absorbed, along with many others, by a contract for eight hundred families to be settled in the same area by Stephen F. Austin and Samuel M. Williams. Through

Headquarters of possibly the only complete plantation unit in Texas
with house, land, slave quarters, stables, and burial grounds

compromises and settlements won in the legal negotiations which ensued, Robertson obtained title to his own lands and was left with considerable holdings in Bell County, as his lands in fee and by empresario bonuses.

Robertson's son, E. Sterling C., was born in Tennessee in 1820. Brought to Texas at the age of twelve, he attended school in San Antonio and acquired a facility in Spanish which later aided him in his services to the state. When he was only fifteen he became a clerk in the land office of the Robertson colony and participated in frontier battles against hostile Indians. In 1836 he was a regular soldier in his father's company and served briefly with the Texas army against Santa Anna.

After the conclusion of the Revolution, the young Robertson returned briefly to Tennessee to complete his education. Back in Texas in 1839, he embarked on a career of service to Texas, becoming first assistant postmaster general and then postmaster general of the Republic. In 1844 General Houston appointed him a colonel of the Second Regiment of Militia. The next year he was admitted to the practice of law, and in 1848 he became Spanish translator in the general office —at that time a position of much importance. In 1848 he was also elected secretary of the Senate.

In 1852 Robertson settled in Bell County on 93,000 acres, 640 of which were given to him for his brief service at San Jacinto. Here at Salado he reared his six sons and six daughters, and became prominent in town, county, and state affairs. In 1858 he was elected chief justice of Bell County, and supervised the building of the first courthouse for the county. He became brigadier general of state troops, and in 1860-61 he represented Bell County as a delegate to the secession convention. During the Civil War he served on the staff of General Henry McCulloch, ending the war with a commission as brigadier general in the Confederate army. He was a delegate to the state constitutional convention of 1875, playing a notable part in championing public education and urging the retention of the homestead provision in state land laws.

Robertson was one of the founders of Salado College. He donated one hundred acres of land to be sold for the college fund. In the gift a special provision was made concerning every Salado lot sold for the fund that "if at any time said lot should be used for saloon purposes," the deed should be rendered null and void and the property should revert to Robertson's estate. Students were to live quiet lives, for there was to be "no horse-riding, no gambling, no bathing in the creek, and no shooting within the town limit."

In the back parlor at the Robertson home, a group of students met to form a literary society known as "Amasavourian" (I Love to Know), which raised $150 by giving a fair at the college and with the money purchased books, which were widely circulated. Together with books chosen from Robertson's classical library, these volumes made up one of the first circulating libraries in Texas.

Today, members of the Robertson family still live in what was once called "Sterling's Castle." Many of the original furnishings are in use in the house, and more than 10,000 priceless documents are on exhibit there, together with rare books, silver and glassware, guns, and china.

Open to visitors by appointment.

The kitchen-dining-service wing, built of native limestone

Six-room slave quarters, intact after a hundred years

The Governor's Mansion

Colorado between West 10th and 11th

THE "WHITE HOUSE OF TEXAS," the Governor's Mansion which stands across the street from the capitol building in Austin, has served the governors of Texas since the 1850's. The gracious two-story brick house, with its stately Ionic columns and double galleries, built after the Greek Revival manner, is one of the state's finest examples of Southern Colonial architecture.

When the city of Austin was laid out, it was as the capital of a sovereign nation. The choice of the site was made by a Capital Commission appointed in 1839 by President Mirabeau B. Lamar. The original thought is credited to Lamar himself; for in 1837, on a hunting trip up the Colorado River, he is said to have reined in his horse on the spot where the capitol building now stands and exclaimed, "How beautiful! How glorious! This should be the seat of a future empire!"

The commission, made up of Albert C. Horton, Louis P. Cooke, Isaac W. Burton, William Menefee, and Isaac Campbell, agreed. In their unanimous report they wrote:

The imagination of even the romantic will not be disappointed on viewing the valley of the Colorado and the woodlands and prairies at a distance from it, and the citizen's bosom will swell with honest pride when, standing at the portico of the capitol of his country, he looks abroad upon a region worthy of being the home of the brave and free.

There was already a very small village at the site. Called Waterloo, it had been founded in 1838 by General Edward Burleson at the foot of what is now Congress Avenue. Because of the danger of Indian attack, however, only half a dozen pioneers had settled there. When in 1840 the Texas Congress confirmed the selection of the site and changed the name to Austin, to honor the "Father of Texas," some $21,000 was paid for a little over 7,000 acres of land.

Workmen who immediately began to cut cedar logs for the first capitol buildings from the brakes near by were protected from possible Comanche attacks by Texas Rangers. The buildings which were then erected were crude, lacking in both beauty and convenience. But the President and the members of his Cabinet, when they rode in from Houston in November, 1839, to occupy them, were greeted with ceremony: festivities included a barbecue and a ball. The official life of the Capital City, begun with these festivities, was carried on in the log buildings until the first permanent capitol building was erected.

In 1846 Texas was annexed by the United States, and governors replaced presidents at the capital. Governor Elisha M. Pease, fourth governor of the state of Texas, together with his wife, the former Lucadia C. Niles, was instrumental in locating the Governor's Mansion on the beautiful site where it stands today, rather than on the site of the old land office, which had been considered first. The Mansion was built in 1853, the year Governor Pease took office, and he and Mrs. Pease were its first occupants.

The Mansion was designed by the Austin pioneer carpenter-architect, Abner Cook. The plan placed on each floor four square rooms around a central hallway; and these rooms, plus a kitchen wing which was built apart from the main portion, composed the original structure. The walls were of brick, and the cedar for woodwork was hauled from Bastrop by slaves. Nine commodious fireplaces provided heat in winter, while wide porches lent comfort during the long Texas summers.

The notable architectural feature of the spacious entrance hall, which runs the length of the original house, is the spiral stairway winding its graceful way to the second floor. The hall is decorated in white and green, with white woodwork, green carpets, and wallpaper in a scroll pattern repeating the two colors. To the right an antique French mirror hangs over a marble console; to the left are two French *causeuses* which

"The Mansion," home of Texas governors since 1853

were once the property of Count Saligny, minister from France to the Republic of Texas in 1840. (These were restored and presented to the Mansion by Emma Kyle Burleson in 1932.) Above these *causeuses* hang portraits of Governor and Mrs. Richard Coke. Other elaborately framed portraits on the walls of the hall are those of John Reagan, William H. Wharton, and John A. Wharton.

The two north rooms, formerly the "front and back parlors," have now been combined into a single formal reception room known as the "Blue Room." Its walls are tinted French blue, with which the dusty rose of the draperies and valances contrasts pleasingly. The two elegant crystal chandeliers are replicas of those in the White House in Washington.

South of the entrance hall is another reception room, the "Green Room." Here green silk velvet valances edged in gold, draperies of imported French brocade, green wall-to-wall carpet, and wallpaper of moss green blocked in antique gold furnish a Victorian background for decorative items such as a lovely pair of whale oil lamps, gifts of Governor and Mrs. Dan Moody. The chandelier, once piped for gas, is the only original light fixture remaining in the Mansion. In front of the marble fireplace are Victorian brass screens. It was in this fireplace, it is said, that Sam Houston burned a letter from Lincoln just before the Civil War.

Directly back of the Green Room is the handsome State Dining Room. Impressively decorated in red with accents of white, the dining room is used for all state luncheons and banquets. The Chinese red, flock design paper above a white dado is matched by the red wall-to-wall carpet. Woodwork and marble of the two fireplaces serve as white accents, as does the beautiful upholstery of the Chippendale dining chairs which surround the commodious mahogany table. Draperies of off-white damask with red fringe frame the tall windows. An ornate crystal chandelier and a massive Chippendale sideboard complete the striking decor of the room.

The south and west wings, which are additions to the original plan of the Mansion, are private rooms of the governor's family. The only part of the Mansion open to the public beyond the rooms described above is the Sam Houston room on the second floor. This historic chamber contains many valuable relics of the early days, such as the often-mentioned Sam Houston mahogany four-poster from Huntsville, which is draped in ruby-red brocaded damask. The draperies are of the same fabric, as is the upholstery of the banquette. In this room stands the mahogany desk, or chest, of Stephen F. Austin which the Father of Texas once used at Peach Point Plantation, the home of his sister, Mrs. Emily M. Perry. This priceless antique was presented to the Mansion by the heirs of James F. Perry, II.

On the wall of the Sam Houston room hangs, framed, the handwritten treaty which Houston concluded with the Cherokee Indians. Here also is Houston's picture, a copy of one by Fredericks of New York executed about 1856 when Houston represented Texas in the Congress of the United States. It was discovered in the home of a Dallas descendant of Anna Raguet, the girl who received the magnolia blossom—"laurels of victory"—from the San Jacinto battlefield. It was presented to the Governor's Mansion by a grandson of Houston, Temple Houston Morrow.

The harmony which prevails in the furnishings of the Mansion did not come about by chance. The original furnishings for the house were purchased in 1854, when Governor Pease sent Colonel S. M. Swenson to New York to procure rugs, draperies, and furniture. As years passed, pieces were added at random according to the mode current at the time, with little thought, at first, of a long-range plan. This haphazard procedure produced a confusing picture, with delicate eighteenth-century French chairs standing alongside massive Victorian chests. In order to remedy the situation a Mansion Board was created, to confer with each governor's wife in the selection of furniture and the redecoration of rooms.

The Mansion has been repaired and modernized by succeeding governors. Each first lady has added or subtracted something. Mrs. Joseph D.

(Above) Double galleries of the Governor's Mansion

(Below) Spacious entrance hall and spiral stairway

Sayers, sometimes known as the "Dolly Madison of Texas," whose husband was governor from 1899 to 1903, removed the fountains from the front yard. Mrs. Thomas Mitchell Campbell (1907-11) took pride in having the yard terraced and sidewalks laid. It was she who, upon revisiting the house in later years, expressed the wish that she might have had the additional room then provided, "so that my daughters wouldn't have had to move every time the Governor brought guests home!"

Others also made contributions. Mrs. James Stephen Hogg (1891-95) was the first to paper the walls, and Governor and Mrs. Charles A. Culberson (1895-99) added a baseburner. Governor and Mrs. Oscar Branch Colquitt (1911-15) supplied an addition, redecorated the library, and built a family dining room. They also added new bathrooms—a phase of the planning of the Mansion that has been a constant source of conversation ever since a part of one porch was enclosed and the first tin tub installed there. (One first lady of Texas remarked that the joke was on anyone who tried to take a bath in the Governor's Mansion. It is a matter of record that for years the Mansion's plumbing was not adequate to furnish water for more than one bath at a time.) Mrs. Pat Neff (1921-25) was responsible for the addition of the sun parlor and the sleeping porches, and Mrs. Ross Sterling (1931-33) left the Mansion the work of her own hands in the form of needlepoint for one of the sofas.

Distinguished guests of the Mansion during its history of more than a century have included President and Mrs. McKinley, Margaret Woodrow Wilson, Lord and Lady Halifax, Lord Randolph Churchill, General Jonathan Wainwright, and many others. While there is no rigid plan of entertainment, one official custom which has been carried on through the years is that of honoring members of the legislature with a reception. Another tradition usually followed is that of the outgoing governor's complimenting the incoming governor with a luncheon immediately following the eleven o'clock inaugural ceremonies. Other official functions vary from one administration to the next.

Like most century-old houses, the Mansion has its ghost story. Tragedy entered its halls when the nephew of Governor Pendleton Murrah, Civil War governor whose administration was terminated by the fall of the Confederacy, committed suicide in the little North Room. Subsequently it was rumored, especially among the servants, that ghostly moanings could be heard in that part of the house and that doors would sometimes open and close apparently of their own volition.

A visit to the Governor's Mansion is both an opportunity to see the best in Texas architecture of its period and a lesson in Texas history. During the hours when the various public rooms of the Mansion are open, visitors are welcomed by a Texas Ranger and guided tours are conducted through the rooms.

The Mansion is open to visitors daily, Monday through Friday, 10 a.m. to 12 a.m., and by special appointment.

The Sam Houston
bedroom

A corner of the
"Blue Room"

Governor Pease House: "Woodlawn"

6 Niles Road

"WOODLAWN," THE HOME of Governor Elisha M. Pease, was designed by the same architect who was responsible for the design of the Governor's Mansion, Abner Cook, and is in the same Greek Revival style. The story of its origin is that during the early 1850's James T. Shaw planned the house with his bride-to-be, a belle of New Orleans. But before the house was completed the girl changed her mind. Shaw married another woman not long after, and to this union a child was born which died in infancy. When death took his wife also, within the year, Shaw quit the house and never entered it again.

Pease had been planning to build on his property, which extended from Twelfth Street to Shaw's property line. But as Mrs. Pease, whom he had married in 1850, liked the beautiful house already situated on the crest of the adjoining wooded acreage, he purchased it from Shaw instead. Some changes were made after the new owner moved in, in 1853. The plain brick of the exterior was painted red, and the wood trim, even to the columns, green.

Mrs. Pease, perhaps influenced by her travels in England and the Continent, painted the white colonial interior woodwork a rich, dark brown. When she converted the downstairs bedroom into a second parlor, she widened the doorway leading from the entrance hall. Part of the stairway then had a double rail, supported by massive hand-carved newels.

The original plan of the house called for a center hallway with three rooms on the left and one on the right, in contrast with the usual arrangement of two rooms on each side. The three first-floor rooms on the left consisted of two parlors and a library, today filled with valuable antiques, among which are marble-topped tables, mahogany and walnut chairs, chests, sofas, and a clock with wooden works, brought by Pease from Connecticut, which is still keeping time.

Altogether the house now comprises twelve large rooms, not including the baths or the kitchen wing.

Pease, who was born in Connecticut in 1812 and educated as a lawyer, is identified with the history of Texas from the time when he served as secretary to the General Consultation at San Felipe in 1835. During the years of the Republic he was first chief clerk of the Texas Navy, then an officer in the Treasury Department, and finally, by appointment of President Houston, Comptroller of Public Accounts. For a time he practiced law in Brazoria.

After Texas became a state, Pease served as a representative in the first and second terms of the legislature and as a senator in the third. In 1853 he was elected governor, in which capacity he served until 1857, defeating in the campaign for his second term the candidate of the Know-Nothing party. During his administration the Texas permanent school fund, now one of the country's greatest endowment funds, was established by the appropriation of $2,000,000 of the $10,000,000 received in settlement of Texas' claim to lands north and west of the present boundaries of the Trans-Pecos and Panhandle regions.

In 1867, Pease was appointed provisional governor by General Sheridan. Those years of the aftermath of the Civil War were exceedingly confused; and in September, 1869, Pease resigned his office in discouragement over the wrangling of the constitutional convention then in session, and its inability to finish its work.

Three generations of the Pease family have occupied the ancestral home. Niles Graham, the present occupant, is a direct descendant of the governor. Today, as in the past, graciousness and friendliness meet the visitor who passes through the open iron gates decorated with the Texas Lone Star.

Two views of "Woodlawn," home of Governor Elisha M. Pease

Neill-Cochran House

2310 San Gabriel

THE NEILL-COCHRAN HOME, one of Austin's most beautiful ante-bellum houses, has the same external appearance today as it had when it was built in the 1850's. The setting in which it stands retains its feeling of serene dignity, though it is not as spacious in measurement as it was at the start. Originally the front yard ran all the way down to what is now Rio Grande Street. Twenty-Third Street, which today dead-ends at the front walk of the old house, was then the driveway leading up to the wide veranda. A white picket fence, with stiles, once enclosed the property.

The towering Doric columns of the house were made in sections in Houston and hauled to Austin by ox teams. At the base of one are inscribed the names of two former owners. In the upstairs windows may be seen the original blue glass. A glance into the wide central hall reveals a graceful winding stairway. White woodwork frames the doors, which swing on handmade hinges and are held together by wooden pegs. Twenty-four-inch partitions which rest on their own foundations, thick walls, high ceilings, and shuttered windows make the house an ideal dwelling in the heat of Texas summers. For winter, a fireplace was provided in every room.

Green Washington Hill, the builder of the home, came to Texas from Columbus, Georgia, with a group of settlers who located in what they later named Columbus, Texas. Colonel Neill purchased the property from Hill, and he and his wife and two children, together with Mrs. Neill's sister and her husband, Mr. and Mrs. F. W. Cashell, occupied the house for a time. After Colonel Neill's death the story spread that the house was haunted, and to this day one can hear it said that after dark "you can see the old Colonel riding on his white horse."

In the 1890's the T. B. Cochrans bought the home. Members of the family reside there today. Mrs. Cochran's daughter married Raymond M. Hill, a relative of the original builder, and so it happens that descendants of Green Washington Hill once again occupy the home that was sold by their pioneer ancestor.

Like many of the large homes scattered over Texas, the Neill-Cochran house played a definite part in the Civil War, as a hospital for Union troops. It is said that many Northern youths lie buried under the building just north of the old house. For a short time after the Civil War the structure served still another purpose, that of housing the Blind Institute.

The Neill-Cochran House

The Former French Legation

San Marcos and East Eighth

THOUGH THE REPUBLIC OF TEXAS was recognized by several nations, France was the only country ever to send an official representative to live in Texas. That representative, Count Alphonse de Saligny, designed and built as his government's Legation in Austin a Provincial French cottage which, now reputedly Austin's oldest house, has stood on its original site since 1841.

The Legation, which Saligny occupied from the spring of 1842 to 1845, was constructed of hand-hewn lumber from Bastrop. Its double doors with huge locks and of barrel design swing on serpentine hinges. Doors, locks, and hinges were all brought from France. Molded architraves frame the doors and windows, both inside and out, and the mantels are notable for their simplicity and refinement.

During Saligny's incumbency, the Legation was the scene of many social affairs. The ample rooms on either side of the hall were elaborately furnished for official entertaining. An attic which was reached by stairs from the hall held a store of supplies, and the wine cellar was well stocked.

But all was not gaiety and harmony at the Legation. The "pig episode," for example, almost caused an international incident. The pigs in question, which belonged to an innkeeper named Richard Bullock, roamed the streets of Austin. The annoyance they caused the citizens was as nothing to the ire of Saligny when they intruded on his orderly premises, uprooting flowers, pushing over fences, exciting the Count's horses, and eating their corn. In a letter to the Secretary of State of Texas, Saligny complained that his servants had used 140 pounds of nails to mend fences torn down by the hogs, three of which had actually entered his chamber, eating towels and destroying papers. When a horse frightened by the hogs trampled one of the French domestics, the Count ordered his servants to go armed, and to kill trespassing swine. When they carried out these orders Bullock attacked a servant with "threats, stones, sticks, and even a hatchet."

After hot words had been exchanged between Count and innkeeper, Saligny, angry because the government of Texas had not taken prompt steps to defend him against the marauders, demanded his passports and sailed for New Orleans, shaking the dust of Texas from his feet. Texas, meanwhile, struggling against overwhelming financial difficulties, had been seeking a loan from France. It so happened that France's Minister of Finances was Saligny's brother-in-law. When he heard the shocking story of the Count's experience with the pigs, the French loan to Texas was refused, and Franco-Texan relations deteriorated.

After the Legation's day of official glory was past, a lattice rail with the legend "Legation of France" was removed from the front of the dormer windows, and a service wing was added. When the house became the property of Dr. Joseph W. Robertson, the new owner hauled furniture for it from Tennessee. Later the hand-painted muslin on the walls was replaced with fine wallpaper.

The cottage was owned and occupied by the Robertson family for many years. In 1945 a bill was passed by the state legislature authorizing the purchase of the estate, and providing that "the Daughters of the Republic of Texas shall operate the property as a museum with the State Board of Control retaining the title." Now the Daughters of the Republic have completed the task of restoration, which included clearing and replanting of the grounds as well as repair and furnishing of the building itself. An incongruous rear wing, not in the French cottage style of the original structure, was removed. When the formal opening of the museum was celebrated on April 5, 1956, the Legation had been faithfully restored to its appearance in the days of the Republic.

Open daily to visitors, 1 p.m. to 6 p.m.

(Right) House before restoration

(Below) Former French Legation, now a
museum operated by the
Daughters of the Republic
of Texas

Northeast Texas

Adolphus Sterne House 211 La Nana

Peter Ellis Bean House Four miles east of Nacogdoches on the Melrose Road

THE ADOLPHUS STERNE HOUSE in Nacogdoches, which has stood more than a century and in 1936 was awarded a Centennial marker as a Texas landmark, was the home of a native of Cologne, Germany, who became a Texas patriot in the days of Mexican rule, one of the wealthiest men in the province, a friend of Sam Houston, and a financier of the Texas Revolution.

The home, which was built in 1830, four years after Sterne settled in East Texas, is occupied and well maintained. It is an ell-shaped clapboard structure with a long, inviting front porch and massive chimneys, which stand detached from the house walls at either end of the front wing. The arrangement of the house affords cross ventilation for most of the rooms. Each door leading from the entrance hall to one of the front rooms features a cross in six panels.

Adolphus Sterne became alcalde, or mayor, of Nacogdoches under the Mexican government. In 1832 he helped to drive from the town the Mexican force which, under Colonel José de las Piedras, had garrisoned it since 1827, and to restore home rule to what was one of the oldest settlements in Texas.

A friendship with Sam Houston, begun earlier in Tennessee, was renewed in Texas, where Sterne often entertained Houston at his home. There, in 1833, Houston was baptized a Catholic, naming as his godmother Mrs. Sterne, the former Eva Rosine Roff, daughter of a Louisiana planter. (At that time, the majority of Texans were at least nominally Catholics, since the Mexican colonization laws required that all colonists profess that faith.) When Houston, as commander in chief of the revolutionary army of Texas, issued his call to arms, Sterne raised thousands of dollars and organized three companies of volunteers to oppose Mexican tyranny.

During the years of the Republic, Sterne served in the Texas Congress. Later he became a mem-

ber of the Texas state legislature, and at one time was postmaster of Nacogdoches. When he died in 1852 he was buried in Nacogdoches, the adopted home which he had served so faithfully.

ON MELROSE ROAD, some four miles east of Nacogdoches, stands one of the several homes of Peter Ellis Bean, "The Ingenious Colonel." Probably built in 1829, the unpretentious ranch-style house gives no hint of the turbulent career of its original owner. One of the two large chimneys at the end of the two front rooms, their tall flues set away from the walls for safety, bears the date of 1848, showing that it was added some time after the house was built—though still over a century ago. Across the front a long porch shelters the entrance to the usual central hall.

Bean, who was born in Tennessee in 1783, was a member of Philip Nolan's filibustering expedition into Texas in 1800-1801, and was the only member of that ill-fated company to regain his freedom after the Spaniards killed Nolan and imprisoned all his men. After twelve years in the Chihuahua prison in Mexico, Bean escaped and joined the Morelos revolution, becoming an officer in the Mexican army.

Sent by the Mexicans to the United States as an envoy in 1814, Bean met pirate Jean Lafitte and went with him to join General Jackson's forces in New Orleans, where he took part in the famous battle against the British. Years of wandering ensued, during which he spent some time in Texas and some in Mexico. He was Mexican commandant at Fort Teran in 1831 and at Nacogdoches from 1832 to 1835. In 1836 he chose to remain a Mexican colonel, and was interned in the Old Stone Fort at Nacogdoches as an alien. Afterward he left Texas and returned to Xalapa, Mexico.

The grounds of the Sterne house are open to visitors; the Bean house is not open.

Home of Adolphus Stern, alcalde of Nacogdoches
under Mexican rule

One of several homes of the colorful Peter Ellis Bean

Colonel Stephen W. Blount House

501 Columbia

TRAVELERS WHO PASSED through San Augustine in the 1840's saw not a frontier village of log cabins and crudely constructed huts, but a town of finely proportioned and beautifully ornamented white homes. The Colonel Stephen W. Blount home, built in 1839, is a splendid example of the small house of classic lines which was to be found at that time in the town now sometimes called "the Williamsburg of Texas."

The Blount house was designed and built by Augustus Phelps, an architect of excellent taste who also built the Cartwright and Cullen houses in San Augustine during the same period. The one-story frame house with its two ells has an entrance porch supported by Doric columns and leading to an arched doorway. The highly decorative cornice of the main portion of the house is also notable. The restful beauty of the structure springs from its having been designed by Phelps according to the classic rules of proportion.

Colonel Blount, original owner of the house, was a Georgian of a distinguished family, his grandfather having fought in the Revolutionary War. He was advised to come to Texas by Archibald Hotchkiss of Nacogdoches, who persuaded him that the state offered rich opportunities. "On his arrival at Alexandria, La.," says George L. Crocket in his *Two Centuries in East Texas,*

he learned from some wagoners that there was a famine of salt meat in San Augustine. Finding a quantity of bacon in Alexandria he loaded a wagon with it and sold it in San Augustine at a small profit, thus giving evidence of business enterprise and public spirit which were marked characteristics of his whole life.

Blount had been in San Augustine only a year when he was chosen as a delegate to the convention at Washington-on-the-Brazos which declared the independence of Texas and adopted a constitution for the Republic. Together with other delegates, he made the journey on horseback. The group rode three days, sleeping at night on the ground, rolled in their blankets. At the convention, Blount was one of the signers of the Texas Declaration of Independence.

On their way home, the delegates from East Texas met a company of men en route to join Houston's main army. They joined the detachment, and arrived at the Battle of San Jacinto just in time to pursue the fleeing Mexicans.

Blount engaged in the mercantile business in San Augustine, where he also served as clerk of the county court and as postmaster. At the age of eighty-two he enjoyed the distinction of being the only surviving signer of the Declaration of Independence.

With the passing of years, the beauty of the Blount house was dimmed. Fortunately, however, in recent years the building was purchased and restored by Raiford L. Stripling, an architect of distinction. The restoration was carried out in the most minute detail. Not only was the original loveliness of the exterior revived, but floors were scraped, successive layers of paper were removed from walls and ceilings, rusty nail holes in old woodwork were plugged and sanded, and new supports were added to walls and floors. The result of the long, laborious, and costly process has been most gratifying to lovers of the fine old homes of Texas.

Open to visitors by appointment.

House before restoration
by architect
Raiford L. Stripling

The Blount house, one of Texas' most beautifully designed and restored homes

Matthew Cartwright House 505 East Main

Phillip A. Sublett House Three miles east of San Augustine

IN 1837, when the Republic of Texas was at its beginning, the pioneers of San Augustine (one of the oldest towns in Texas, since the first Anglo-Americans arrived there in 1818 and the town was founded in 1832) incorporated the San Augustine University, which a decade later merged with Wesleyan College into the University of Eastern Texas. Across the street from the university, Isaac Campbell built in 1839 a dignified colonial house. Campbell, who was named one of the committee to select the site for the city of Austin, moved from San Augustine a short time later, and the house was used for classes of Wesleyan College until the school's permanent building was completed.

In 1847 Matthew Cartwright purchased the home, which has remained through the years in the possession of his family. It is a finely proportioned two-story frame house with an ell at the back. Huge fireplaces at either end of the main structure bespeak comfort, and the column-supported entrance porch is of classic simplicity.

Matthew Cartwright came to Texas from Tennessee with his parents at the age of fourteen. The family stopped about six miles east of San Augustine. When the town of San Augustine was planned, the Cartwrights moved their store into town under the name of John Cartwright and Son. In the Texas Revolution, the younger Cartwright participated in the siege of Bexar and the Battle of Concepcion. A cavalryman at San Jacinto, he had a horse shot from under him in the skirmish of April 20, the day before the final battle.

Cartwright was one of the few men of his time in East Texas to recognize the value of land. He bought many of the land certificates to which each married man was entitled under the early laws of colonization. Thus, when the fertile lands were settled and their value increased he amassed a fortune. He enlarged the family store at the northeast corner of San Augustine's public square, and for many years carried on an extensive mercantile business there. Known for his fairness, he lent his support to many worthy enterprises for the enrichment of the life of his community.

EAST OF SAN AUGUSTINE are many old settlements, one of which is the Sublett Place. Phillip A. Sublett, son-in-law of Elisha Roberts, paid a squatter fifty dollars for his rights to this property when he came to Texas in 1824. The present Sublett house, built about 1850, stands today in a good state of preservation. It is a commodious structure with a long ell running to the rear. The general arrangement of the house is typical of the period in which it was constructed, the two end chimneys serving both lower and upper floors. The entrance door is distinguished by an attractive decorative molding.

A staunch friend of Sam Houston, Sublett was chairman of the Committee of Safety which in 1835 nominated Houston as commander in chief of the Department of Nacogdoches. This appointment led to Houston's subsequent nomination as commander of all Texas forces.

When Houston called for volunteers, Sublett, as lieutenant colonel and second in command, led a group of men from San Augustine. These soldiers became part of the force that fought furiously from house to house—even from room to room—at San Antonio, until the Mexican army under General Cos surrendered unconditionally. After the Battle of San Jacinto Houston, who was en route to New Orleans, stopped at Sublett's home to rest and recuperate to some degree from the wound he had received in the battle.

The Sublett house is open to visitors.

(Above and left) Two views of the Matthew Cartwright house

(Below) Home of Phillip A. Sublett

Judge Ezekiel W. Cullen House

Market and Congress

A PARTICULARLY NOTABLE FEATURE of the Judge Ezekiel W. Cullen home, built in 1839 in the Greek Revival style, is the use of the Texas Star, which centers the double-door molding and also the downspouts at either end of the porch. The use of the Lone Star in the tin gutters of the house is identical with that found in the old Stage Coach Inn at Chappell Hill. The porch gable is supported by Doric columns, and interesting panel decorations such as are usually seen only in interiors surround the windows. The simple one-story house is one of the loveliest of its type standing in Texas today.

Of generous proportions considering its one-story design, the Cullen house originally boasted an attic extending the whole length and breadth of the house, and finished as a ballroom.

After participating in the siege of Bexar in 1835, the original owner of this fine home began a distinguished career in law. Judge Cullen was a representative from San Augustine County in the Third Congress of the Republic of Texas. In 1839 he served as judge of the First District. In 1850, when General Zachary Taylor was President, Cullen was appointed purser of the United States Navy. He left San Augustine to take up his duties in this position, living for the next twenty years in Pensacola, Florida, and in Washington, D.C.

After the Civil War the Cullen house became the property of the Elisha Roberts family. Benjamin Roberts, the actual owner, was the son of Elisha, who was a member of the committee of sixteen which selected the site of the present town of San Augustine. He was also one of the incorporators of the University of San Augustine.

The story is told that in 1822 Elisha Roberts, on the trail of a slave who became a runaway when his wife was taken to Central Texas by another slaveholder, passed through the place where San Augustine now stands. Impressed with the countryside, he resolved that one day he would return to it. Later, when his slave ran away a second time, Roberts once more pursued him and this time noted a squatter who was occupying the exact spot he had admired before. Wasting no time, Roberts returned to his family and moved them, along with all his household effects, to the new location to which he had been led by his desire to retrieve his slave.

A few years ago Hugh Roy Cullen, grandson of Judge Cullen, purchased the property and restored the residence. In 1953 he presented it to the San Augustine Chapter of the Daughters of the Republic of Texas. Now the house, in all its original beauty, is open to both visitors and local civic groups. It has been furnished with fine antiques, one of the most interesting of which is a mahogany wardrobe once owned by Sam Houston and kept by him at the capitol in Austin during his governorship, for the storage of his uniforms.

During the spring and summer the house is open to visitors on alternate Sundays, and at other times by appointment. There is no admission fee, but a donation is welcome.

Home of Judge Ezekiel W. Cullen, presented by his grandson to the
San Augustine Chapter of the Daughters of the Republic of Texas

William Garrett House Two miles west of San Augustine

Johnson House: Old Halfway Inn Two miles west of Chireno

ON DECEMBER 31, 1854, Mary Garrett wrote home to Texas from New Jersey, where she had been sent to school:

. . . this is a very lonesum place although there is so many girls. . . . Pa, you must be sure and come after me. . . . Just to think of *Home* that sweet place home pa you do not know how much we suffer here it is so hard for us to stay . . . you must excuse all mistakes and the bad writing and write immediately to your daughter.

The letter was written to William Garrett, who after moving to Texas first established a store at Nacogdoches, then went to Ayish Bayou, and finally settled west of San Augustine. In 1861 he built there a house so generously proportioned that it might have been patterned after his homesick daughter's dream. Its double-entrance doorway is flanked by side lights the width of the doors themselves. The dormers in the roof are oversized, as are the twelve-light windows of the first floor. In every detail of its appearance, the house is broad and welcoming and homelike.

William Garrett's father, Jacob Garrett, followed him from Arkansas. He took up a grant of land on the Attoyac River which in later years grew to be one of the largest plantations in the country. He also purchased and lived in the Thomas McFarland home, seven miles west of San Augustine. (This home is not now standing, but its site is indicated by a granite marker.) Jacob Garrett took a prominent part in the birth of the Texas Republic. He was not only a delegate to the first convention which met in 1832 at San Felipe to petition the Mexican government for the redress of numerous grievances, but also a member of the Consultation which in 1835 formed a provisional Texas government, and a representative from San Augustine in the Permanent Council.

Mrs. Mattie Garrett lived for many years in the William Garrett house. Quite recently the home was bought by Sam Parker, who now owns and occupies it.

IN THE DAYS when the stagecoach carried passengers and mail between San Augustine and Nacogdoches on the Camino Real, the home built near Chireno in the early 1840's by James B. Johnson of San Augustine was used as a halfway station. Here passengers were fed and fresh horses were substituted for the tired ones that had been drawing the coach.

The house was built on the popular plan of a wide center hallway with four rooms surrounding it. To the right, on the first floor, were the living room and kitchen, to the left two bedrooms. The end of the hall served as a dining room. Upstairs more bedrooms and storage space were provided. The house was roomy enough to accommodate overnight guests and thus used as an inn, as were many other Texas homes of that time which were located on well-traveled stage routes.

The owner, a native Virginian, was twice mayor of San Augustine—once at the beginning of the town's history about 1837, and again when it was reincorporated after the Civil War. It is said that he lived in several homes in San Augustine, all close to the square. A restless man who slept poorly, he often circled the business district at night to see if everything was in order, and on several occasions earned the gratitude of the citizenry by spotting, on these nightly strolls, fires that might, but for him, have proved disastrous to the town.

Chireno has a place in Texas history as the town near which the state's first oil well was drilled in 1866. Oil had appeared on the waters of Oil Springs, and so it was decided that a well should be drilled. The well went down only one hundred feet, but that was far enough for it to strike oil.

Both of these houses are open to visitors.

Old Halfway Inn, a stage
stop between Nacogdoches
and San Augustine

The William Garrett house

A. T. Monroe House 400 South Seventh

Monroe-Coleman-Crook House 707 East Houston

ABOUT 1850 Armistad Thompson Monroe, the great-nephew of President James Monroe, built in Crockett a beautiful home which is standing today. It is a spacious two-story residence with wide porches and a deck with entrances from the upper floor. A decorative railing on the roof suggests a "widow's walk" or a frontier lookout.

Monroe was the only one of his Virginia family, of which he was the oldest son, to come West. When he was eighteen he arrived on Galveston Island. Still traveling by boat, he went on to Liberty and then to Alabama Crossing on the Trinity River. Here, in 1846, he met and married the daughter of Jacob Allbright.

Later Monroe moved to Crockett, to become one of its pioneer merchants. In the initial issue of the *Crockett Printer* dated December 8, 1853, he advertised his stock of merchandise. Monroe's name appears often in the records of Houston County. In 1851, along with other prominent citizens of Crockett, he petitioned the Texas legislature for authority of the county court to levy a special tax for the construction of a courthouse. He was a delegate to the 1868 constitutional convention. He was also treasurer of the Trinity Chapter, No. 4, of the Royal Arch Masons, which "held convocations at the Masonic Hall in the Town of Crockett, on the first Monday in each month at 3 o'clock P.M."

Monroe's son, A. T. Monroe, Jr., tells a story of the problems raised by innovations in household equipment in the early days:

My father had the first wood cook stove that was in Houston County, and had it put up at home, but the negro cook said she couldn't cook on that thing, and the only way he could get her to use it was to have the fireplace walled up. After that she would sneak out to her cabin and cook things in the fireplace. It took our family a long time to get her to use the stove.

The exterior of the Monroe home remains unchanged. The interior has been remodeled to suit the requirements of the funeral home which now occupies the building.

THE FINELY PROPORTIONED home of Daniel Coleman, which remains in a splendid state of preservation, was built in 1854 on what is now East Houston Street in Crockett. The lumber for its construction was hauled from Shreveport and sawed and dressed by hand. The framework of the house was hand hewn of oak, and the "boarding over" was cut from good heart-lumber. Under the weatherboarding is brick and behind that lathing for plaster, which was never applied. The original chimneys, built by an early-day brick mason, still stand.

In 1851 Nancy Dean Coleman and her four boys left Alabama and came to Texas. Daniel, one of the sons, founded a plantation a few miles south of Crockett. Some seven or eight years later "Uncle Dan," as he came to be called, moved to town. He purchased the house, which A. T. Monroe had built, and lived there until 1880. Then he went to Henderson County, where he lived with his brother Nat until his death. He had married Louisa Matlock before he came to Texas. Although they had a large family, only three children lived in the home in Crockett.

In 1911 the house became the property of George W. Crook, a widely respected citizen of Crockett and a Mason of high standing. His descendants still live in the strongly built old home.

Neither of these houses is open to visitors.

George W. Crook home, built in 1854

House built by Armistad Monroe, great-nephew of President Monroe

H. R. Link House

1003 North Link

CLOSELY ASSOCIATED with the beautiful Dogwood Trails of Palestine and its environs, visited by large numbers of tourists each spring during the season when the dogwood is in bloom, is the Link home. The white clapboard mansion is today one of the finest old homes in Texas.

Dr. H. H. Link was born in Washington County, Tennessee, and attended the Medical Institute in Cincinnati. After teaching school for a short time in Alabama, he came to Texas in the spring of 1846. For several years he lived in the settlement of old Fort Sam Houston, near the present town of Palestine; and at this time he decided to make Palestine his home. He returned to Louisville, Kentucky, and graduated in medicine there. Then in 1851 he married Miss Hypatia Megee in Indiana and took her to Palestine.

The doctor and his new wife chose the timberlands of the dogwood as their homestead. They were among the first settlers of the new town, now called old Palestine, and they built in the midst of lands through which the Dogwood Trail now winds. Their first home was a two-room structure which was later incorporated in the enlarged house as a kitchen. Surrounded by a fruit orchard, the old home stood on the Link land, which extended all the way down the Dogwood Trail.

In this home the three Link boys and one daughter were born. All the Link sons were educated in Virginia. John Link attended Washington University when General Robert E. Lee was its president; and on the desk in President Lee's office, which is preserved as he left it, is the roll of the Latin class which contains John Link's name. The three sons became doctors and were associated with their father in the practice of medicine in and around Palestine. For nearly a century the Link family furnished doctors for the town and its environs. Dr. H. R. Link, "Dr. Henry," who inherited the old Link place, was associated with his brother E. W., "Dr. Ed," during the last years of their lives.

The Link mansion was raised and remodeled in 1912 by Dr. H. R. Link and is still cherished and preserved as a memorial to the family. Of Greek Revival architecture, the stately home has a spacious front porch, its roof supported by six Ionic columns. The curved extension of the upper balcony, between the two center columns, is supported by two smaller columns of the same order. Green shutters flank the stained-glass windows of the front rooms. The imposing doorway opens into a large hall from which rises a fine stairway leading to the upper rooms.

A graveled driveway leads through the grove of ancient cedars and elms by the side of the dwelling past the large ell, which contains the original house. A fan-shaped porch in the rear gives privacy to the occupants and affords a fine view. The winding driveway continues past the trees to an old carriage house. In the yard on the north side of the residence is a moss-covered rockery, the stones in which came from the original foundation of the old home.

The house is well preserved and appropriately furnished. Some of Dr. H. H. Link's original possessions still remain in the rooms—among them a bureau, a spool bed, flat silver, and a secretary similar to one in Sam Houston's home in Huntsville.

Some of the Link land was sold and now forms part of the Dogwood Trails, which are composed of lands, parks, and drives, some privately owned and some the property of Anderson County. Part of the land has been given in easement by heirs who now own the E. W. Link estate.

The Link mansion, continuously occupied by members of the Link family since the first portion of it was built, forms both a worthy monument to the memory of its founder and a historic approach to the scenic Dogwood Trails.

Open daily to visitors, in the mornings.

H. R. Link home, synonymous
with the Dogwood Trail

Alexander-McNaughton House 407 East Kolstad

Gooch House 710 Perry

ONE OF THE OLDEST houses in Palestine is the Alexander home, built in 1848 on Judge John B. Mallard's plantation, which adjoined the land owned by Dr. H. H. Link. The low white structure originally consisted of two front rooms with a connecting hall. An ell of more recent date has been added at the rear.

The solid oak foundation was taken from trees on the forested plantation. As nails—except for hand-wrought square spikes—were nonexistent in those pioneer days, the heavy beams for the foundation were put together with pegs. Many of the heavy timbers were mortised to make strong corners and joints. Years later, the razing of the old barns and slave cabins on the plantation was made difficult by the strength of the timbers and pegged beams. And later still, special tools were required to penetrate the eighteen-inch beams in order that plugs for electricity might be placed.

As in many other early homes, the two substantial chimneys which heated the large rooms were not fastened to the walls above the fireboxes, but as a safeguard against fires extended free through the gables. One of these chimneys is still standing. The large fireplace openings, skilfully built to provide good drafts, were framed with nicely milled mantels.

The front porch of the house has simple columns in front with half-columns at the wall. The large hall, lighted by side lights in the front entrance, is now comfortably used as a living room. One heavy original door, of vertical panels, leads to the new addition to the house.

Judge William Alexander married the widow of Judge Mallard, and the Mallard and Alexander heirs lived in the old home for many years. One of the descendants, Frank Eppner, still lives at another address in Palestine. In time a florist named McNaughton bought the house and lived there for many years, beautifying the grounds with flowers and shrubs. Mrs. Maggie Miller is the present owner.

ANOTHER early-day home of Palestine is the little red house just north of the square often known as the Egan house, but particularly associated with the Gooch family. It is a one-and-a-half-story house constructed of solid brick. From the front it has the look of a small building, but to the rear there are additional wings and ells. The house was built in 1852 by the Masons to house the female department of the Masonic Institute, a pioneer educational institution. This was the first girls' school building in Palestine.

In 1833 Elder Daniel Parker had circumvented the Mexican laws against establishment of Protestant churches in Texas by organizing the Pilgrim Predestinarian Regular Baptist Church in Illinois and escorting the entire congregation to what later became Palestine. But it remained for John Graham Gooch to organize in this house the first Sunday School in the county. Gooch arrived in Texas in the early 1850's, and on his first Sunday in Palestine invited all who were interested to come to the little red house on Perry Street. He subsequently became superintendent of the Sunday School which was formed that day.

Gooch also served as trustee of the Palestine Female Institute, founded in 1858 with money contributed by the people of Palestine and housed in a building on the ground now occupied by the Junior High School. Still another of his educational activities was the starting of a circulating library with books from his own collection.

John Graham Gooch had three sons—John Young, Gideon, and Lucius—all of whom became lawyers and served the community in their different fashions, taking prominent parts in the religious, political, and financial development of Palestine.

The Alexander-McNaughton house is open to visitors on Sundays during the Dogwood Trails.

Gooch or Egan house, built for a girls' school in 1852

Alexander-McNaughton house: a solid oak foundation

Kinnard House

814 South Fourth

THE CITY of Waco took its name from the Waco Indians, a friendly tribe whose village of Waco Springs, kept by the Indians under a treaty with Stephen F. Austin until they were driven out by the Comanches about 1837, was located at what is now the corner of Sixth and Barron Streets. The present city was laid out by Major George B. Erath in 1849.

Many of the fine old homes of Waco were built on Fourth Street. Some of these have disappeared as the city grew—among them the Maddin house, known for its beautiful windows; the Downs home, the town's first two-story house; the Leland house, home of Waco's first postmaster; and the brick home of music-store owner Seymour Ash. But the home completed by John S. Napier in the early 1860's and now known as the Kinnard house still stands.

The back part of the house, built of native brick before the Civil War, is now used as the kitchen for the main house, constructed of similar materials, which was added later. The bricks, made in a kiln near Waco, were burned and glazed to produce the mellow beauty of this old mansion.

Today the grounds are enclosed by a white picket fence, and the house is surrounded by a grove of oak and elm trees and by a profusion of shrubs. Tall Ionic columns support the roof of a two-story porch with an ornamental second-story balcony. The white woodwork of the porch and windows and the green of the shutters offer pleasing contrasts with the red brick of the walls. Fireplaces at either end, built in the fashion of the day, heated four large rooms on each floor. The front door is surrounded by side lights which give light for the front hall and the stairway. Flower circles, lined with brick, decorate the yard from front to back. An old brick well and a brick smokehouse in the back yard show many years of use. Even the old porcelain knocker on the front door contributes to the general atmosphere of antiquity.

The Kinnard home is frequently known as the John Baylis Earle house, having at one time been the residence of the Earles. Eliza Harrison married Dr. John Baylis Earle, pioneer physician of McLennan County. Their son, John Baylis Earle, who was a distinguished graduate of the University of Mississippi, came to Texas in 1855 to settle down.

During the Civil War, the younger Earle ran the Federal blockade with machinery for a cotton gin which provided the impetus for the economic development of Waco. He was a charter member of the Waco Suspension Bridge Company which built a bridge across the Brazos. He died in 1869 before seeing the full fruition of his work for the city.

The Kinnard house, which is furnished with family heirlooms, is now occupied by Miss Mary Kinnard, granddaughter of the builder.

The Kinnard house is not open to visitors.

Kinnard home, frequently known as the John Baylis Earle house

General Thomas Harrison House

800 South Fourth

DIRECTLY ACROSS the street from the Kinnard home is the Harrison-Earle house, generally known as the General Thomas Harrison home. Mrs. Eliza Earle Thompson, who built the house before the Civil War, later sold it to her cousin, Thomas Harrison, with whose family it was identified for many years.

A colonial mansion showing the Greek Revival influence, the two-story structure of white clapboards is notable for the stately Doric columns, the full two stories high, which support the roof of a great porch extending across the entire front and south sides of the house. The fine timbers for this home, like those for a number of other dwellings of its day, were brought by oxcart from Houston. Many of its strong beams and "steadyings" were hand hewn from the cedar and oak groves in the river bottoms. The house was provided with the finest furniture and the best fixtures available. The one bathroom on the back porch boasted a tin tub, set inside a wooden container.

The Harrison home was admirably located in the midst of a large plot of land, facing the Brazos River on the east. The grounds included several acres which, with the growth of the city of Waco, have since become business property. On the lawn with its masses of flowers and shrubs the neighborhood children played with the Harrison children and with the Kinnard children from across the street.

Thomas Harrison, the well-educated son of a southern planter, came to Texas in 1843 and joined a law firm in Brazoria. In 1846 he joined the Mississippi Rifles in the Mexican War, serving a year under Colonel Jeff Davis. In 1847 he returned to Texas and resumed his law practice, first in Houston and later in Marlin. In 1855 he moved to Waco, where he practiced law the rest of his life.

This peaceful career was, however, interrupted by further military service. In 1860 Harrison was elected captain of a Waco company which was sent by Governor Sam Houston to stop raiding Indians. The next year he was chosen to command a cavalry company which became a part of Terry's Rangers. He was twice promoted for bravery on the battlefields of the Civil War, and, having attained the rank of general, distinguished himself in the Battle of Shiloh in the Tennessee Campaign.

After the war General Harrison returned to his fine home in Waco. In 1866 he became the judge in his district, and in 1872 was named a presidential elector. He died in Waco, a much respected citizen and patriot.

The General Thomas Harrison house is not open to visitors.

The Harrison house, one of Waco's finest old homes

Patterson Home

1311 West Oakwood

THE LAND upon which the Patterson home in Tyler stands was acquired by John Lollar, its first owner, in an interesting fashion. Lollar proved to the Board of Land Commissioners for the County of Nacogdoches that, being a married man and having arrived in Texas subsequent to the date of the Texas Declaration of Independence, he was entitled by law to 1,280 acres of land. He further stated that he had resided in the Republic three years and that he had performed all the duties of a citizen. His application having been approved, he was granted a Letter-Patent, dated December 1, 1846, and signed by Governor Pinckney Henderson, Texas' first governor after annexation.

Lollar was one of a committee of five who helped select the site for the town of Tyler. A warranty deed dated February 6, 1848, gives evidence of the fact that one hundred acres were purchased from Edgar Pollitt for the sum of $150 for the county seat of Smith County. This county had been organized from Nacogdoches County. The name of Tyler was selected for the town in honor of John Tyler, tenth President of the United States.

When the town had been laid out, Lollar is said to have built the first house within its city limits. This structure, which was located on North Broadway, later burned. Lollar started the house that now stands on the Oakwood property, and then in 1854 sold the place to J. C. Moore. In

1871 Moore's executor transferred the property, consisting of 364 acres of land and all personal property located on it, to J. M. Patterson for a consideration of $3,100 in gold.

The new owner made some additions to the house. Then in 1880 it was bought by his brother, J. P. Patterson, who in 1882 completely remodeled it. This explains the very definite Victorian look of the house in its present state. The decorated posts, the wood trim around the gables, and the ironwork over the windows were probably added at the time of the remodeling.

In the grounds around the house are some very old shrubs. Some of the rosebushes are said to have bloomed continuously for the past sixty years.

Members of the Patterson family have been numerous in Tyler for many years. John M. Patterson came to the town as early as 1848 and became a leading businessman there. Julius Saunders, a stepson, made an excellent record in Douglas' Texas Battery in the Confederate army, beginning as a private and achieving a lieutenant's commission. Thomas Patterson, a businessman, and Fred Patterson, who served as a tax collector, were other members of the family who made their homes in Tyler.

The Patterson home is now owned and occupied by Mrs. Pearl Patterson.

The Patterson home is not open to visitors.

Built in the 1850's, and since 1871 occupied by the Patterson family

Goodman House: "Bonnie Castle"

624 North Broadway

BEFORE THE CIVIL WAR Samuel Gallatin Smith, a well-to-do bachelor of Tyler, built a four-room house on a knoll among the rocks and trees of his nine acres, and named it "Bonnie Castle." Before going to war as a Confederate captain, Smith sold the place to F. N. Gary, who in turn conveyed it to Dr. Samuel A. Goodman.

Dr. Goodman was a Tennessean, a neighbor of Andrew Jackson and a close friend of Sam Houston. When he retired in 1857 from the practice of medicine in South Carolina, he moved to Texas. With him came his son, Dr. W. J. Goodman, who studied medicine in New York, was attached as surgeon to the 13th Division in the Civil War, and practiced medicine in Tyler for a total of thirty years.

In 1872 the younger Dr. Goodman bought the house on North Broadway from his father for three thousand gold dollars, as a home to which to bring his bride, Priscilla Gaston Goodman. The story is told that after Dr. Goodman had carried his bride across the threshold he placed her in a chair and casually remarked, "Now I have to make a call!" Thus Priscilla learned early what it was to be a doctor's wife.

The house was enlarged and remodeled from time to time, and as the years went by it was the setting for many social affairs. The Goodmans entertained extensively, and often as many as four hundred guests were invited to dance to orchestras brought from as far away as Waco and Dallas. During the early days of Tyler's history much of the life of the community centered around the Goodman home.

The three Goodman children—Etta, Will, and Sallie—were reared in this house. The year 1920 was a sad one for the family. That year Mrs. Goodman died and Etta, who never completely recovered from the shock, died only a few weeks later. Sallie, who was by then Mrs. J. H. LeGrand, became the guardian of the home. Because of the shadow cast by the death of her mother and sister,

the social life connected with the house was less extensive than before.

Mr. LeGrand, a Virginian by birth and grandson of the organizer of the First Baptist Church in Appomattox, served as usher in Tyler's First Baptist Church for forty years. He was a stockholder in a large wholesale grocery firm, and he and Mrs. LeGrand gave liberally to charity.

With the passing of years Mrs. LeGrand's husband and brother were taken by death. Mrs. LeGrand herself was injured in a fall. Having a desire to preserve the old family home and envisioning the encroachment upon it of the growing business section of the town, she wrote a will bequeathing the palatial house and eight wooded acres to the city of Tyler for use as a museum and community center.

A provision of the will which indicates Mrs. LeGrand's concern for every detail of the home and grounds is her bequest of three camellia plants, originally owned by her mother and cherished for many years by the family, to her sister-in-law, Mrs. Will Goodman, and Miss Annie Pruitt. Included in the bequest was a fund for the maintenance of the plants.

Today the Goodman-LeGrand house contains many relics of the past, such as hand-carved poster beds, a spool cradle, a complete wedding trousseau, fine silver, Limoges and Canton china, and rare fans. An unusual item is a series of three "pill cases" used by the pioneer doctors Samuel A. and W. J. Goodman as modes of travel changed: a saddlebag, a medicine box for the buggy, and finally a medicine case to be carried in the early-day automobile.

And today, as in its early years, "Bonnie Castle" is a center of festivity as Tyler celebrates in its rooms many important social and community events.

Open daily to visitors.

Two views of the Goodman house, now a museum and community center

Frazier-Adair House 409 West Grand

Hall-Gwynne-Anderson House: "Mont Hall"

Four miles west on Old Longview Road

IN THE EARLY 1840's Judge George B. Atkins built for his friend, Judge Charles A. Frazier, a house at the west end of what is now Grand Street but was then called Border, one of the borderlines of the original Marshall township. Marshall, named for Chief Justice John Marshall, was located on land originally owned by pioneer settlers Peter and Dicey Whetstone. Whetstone, it is said, thoughtfully placed on his property a jug of whiskey for the encouragement of the committee surveying locations for the townsite.

The Frazier house is one of Marshall's oldest dwellings in continuous use. The story-and-a-half brick house is an adaptation to the terrain of the "raised cottage" style. In the beginning the basement was used as the kitchen and dining room. Two ells have been added to the two-level rear, but aside from minor additions the white brick residence remains structurally intact.

Judge Atkins, the builder, was the first justice of the county, appointed by President Lamar. He arrived in Port Caddo in 1837, and two years later journeyed to Marshall. In 1857 he constructed the Capitol Hotel, which became a famous hostelry of its time, and which he himself operated for many years. He also built the Masonic Institute, the structure which housed Marshall University, and a courthouse which was called "The Little Virginia Courthouse" because of its distinct southern flavor.

From the Frazier family the home which Judge Atkins built for them passed into the hands of the Raineys. Later it was purchased by W. A. Adair, who for fifty years was the editor of the *Evening Messenger*. Dr. Richard Granbery now occupies the house.

"MONT HALL" is located on Hall's Hill, west of Marshall. According to a survey conducted by the University of Texas, Hall's Hill Valley was at one time the bed of a river. The small hills scattered about, thought by many to be Indian mounds, are now believed to be parts of a very ancient river dam. Geological investigations substantiate the view that most of this land was once covered by water. Even today marine shells and fossils are frequently found on the highest hills, notably at Hysons Springs.

Montraville J. Hall, who was known as "Mont," built the house named for him in 1844 or 1845. The property was originally the G. W. Morgan survey, patented under the Texas laws. The county deed records for March, 1844, show that Hall purchased the tract of land, some 640 acres, from Clark and Barton, administrators of the estate of Benjamin Barton, who had lived on the property until his death. Hall bought the land for $1,000, due in twelve months and secured by William Hall (probably Montraville Hall's father) and John B. Hall.

The color of the brick of the two-story residence which Hall erected and the detail work of its entrance, with its two-story columns and second-floor balcony, are distinguishing marks of a century-old house. It is one of the few antebellum homes that remain standing in the Marshall area.

The house was later owned by the Rev. W. H. Carter, Sr., who farmed the land, raising food for his family and feed crops for his extensive herds of cattle. Carter lived to be ninety-three years old, but sold "Mont Hall" many years before his death.

Mrs. Blanche Gwynne, daughter of Mr. Carter, and her husband, Monte Gwynne, came into possession of the old homestead and lived there many years.

The present owner, Mrs. Leala Anderson, has added a few modern features to the house, which is sometimes called "Edgemont" by the Anderson family. Structurally, however, the old dwelling remains the same as in its early days.

Neither house is open to visitors.

Frazier-Adair house, built in the early 1840's

"Mont Hall," named for its builder, Montraville J. Hall

Scott House Eight miles east of Marshall at Scottsville

Andrews House Three miles southwest of Karnack

BEFORE THE CIVIL WAR, the Scott plantation home was the headquarters of the largest slaveholder in Harrison County. William Thomas Scott, who was born in Mississippi, went in 1834 to Louisiana, where he married Mary Rose. The same year they migrated to Texas. Soon after they had crossed into Texas they stopped at a spring and set up their plantation, one of five that eventually came under their supervision.

Two log houses preceded the elevated frame house which was erected in 1840, and which still stands in a good state of preservation. The house is surrounded today by many of the original plants and shrubs brought from Louisiana and planted by Mary Rose Scott. Notable is a majestic rosebush, over a hundred years old, which still blooms luxuriantly each spring.

Scott had a deep interest in politics. He served as representative in the Congress of the Republic, and later in the state legislature. He was a member of the secession convention, and during the ensuing struggle equipment from his plantation aided the Confederacy. With the freeing of the slaves his fortunes were almost wrecked, but he still took an active part in politics, returning to the legislature in 1878.

Soon after he arrived in Texas Scott built a combination school and church, donating the land near his home. The first crude building was later replaced by a frame structure, and this in turn was succeeded by a stone chapel built by Mrs. Elizabeth Scott Youree of Shreveport, Louisiana, who dedicated it to William Scott Youree, an engineer who died in Monterrey, Mexico. The oldest grave in the cemetery near by is that of Mrs. Catherine Scott, grandmother of William Scott, who was buried in 1842.

The old Scott homestead has been incorporated in the Bettie Scott Youree Park Foundation and is now occupied by the local superintendent. A tall granite marker at the front gate commemorates the founding of the town of Scottsville in 1834 by William Thomas Scott, "Pioneer Statesman."

"THE FIRST BRICK HOUSE" is a much disputed phrase in the Marshall area. Some think that the Andrews homestead on the Marshall-Karnack Highway is the oldest, its bricks having been made in a kiln on the place. At any rate, the beautiful white brick structure, standing on a red hill and surrounded by ancient cedars and a white iron fence, is one of the earliest homes built in this neighborhood.

The columned entrance of the Andrews home, with its side lights and balcony, is typical of the more imposing houses of the day. But the windows are unusual, both for their narrowness and for the extra-wide molding that frames them. The stout and lofty ceilings, fashioned from hand-planed twelve-inch boards, are noteworthy.

This manorial house was built by slaves in the mid-nineteenth century for Milt Andrews, a large landowner who combined farming with merchandising. After serving in the Texas Revolution, Andrews managed the Haggerty store at Port Caddo. Major C. K. Andrews, later owner of the house, was county clerk of Harrison County in the early days of its organization, and figured in a complicated dispute over that office which arose from confusion in the designation of the county seat.

For about fifty years the C. K. Andrews home has been occupied by the T. J. Taylor family. Several years ago the house was completely modernized, in such a way that it was made into a comfortable present-day dwelling while its fundamental qualities of good workmanship and sturdy construction were preserved.

The Scott house is not open to visitors.

Andrews house, built of brick made on the plantation

Ante-bellum plantation home of William Thomas Scott,
largest slaveholder in Harrison County

Old Presbyterian Manse

211 Delta

THE OLDEST RESIDENCE still standing in its entirety in Jefferson is the Old Presbyterian Manse, which was built in 1839—only three years after the founding of the Bayou City. Its builder was General James Harrison Rogers, who practiced law in Jefferson both before and after the Civil War. General Rogers was remembered gratefully for his having opened a law library which was available to prominent lawyers of East Texas and to promising students who read law in his office.

Located on Cypress Bayou, Jefferson was in its early days the terminus for sidewheelers which brought freight and passengers from St. Louis and New Orleans. During its heyday in the 1870's, when steamboats plied on Caddo Lake and wagon trains swapped loads along crowded docks, Jefferson promoted trade of more than $10,000,000 annually. As a Texas port, it was second only to Galveston. Even in 1860, a decade before its fullest development had been reached, Jefferson exported 100,000 bales of cotton to Galveston's 140,000.

An iron post supporting a large wheel, which until recently stood at the corner of the Old Manse property, was a reminder of those days when Jefferson was the metropolis of East Texas. The stout buffer was needed when ox wagons, heavily laden with cotton or supplies, cut away the ground as they rounded this corner in following the most direct route to the boat landings.

But Jefferson's booming days as a river port were numbered. When Jay Gould brought his railroad to East Texas and approached Jefferson to secure right of way for the Texas and Pacific, the town—blindly loyal to its waterways—snubbed him. Irate, Gould built the railroad around Jefferson and drew business to new centers. Meanwhile the natural barrier which made the Big Cypress navigable to the port of Jefferson was destroyed, and soon cypress knees choked a silted morass. Warehouses were abandoned, wharves decayed, and the fortunes of Jefferson declined.

Nevertheless, the town refused to die. To replace the vanished trade of the port it has developed lucrative, if less spectacular, local industries. But it still treasures, as reminders of earlier and more expansive days, the Old Manse and other gracious homes built before Jay Gould's private railroad car, "Atalanta" (which, ironically enough, now rests across the busy street from the Excelsior Hotel), rolled haughtily past the stubborn city.

The Old Manse, a notable example of the Greek Revival style as applied to a one-story frame house, is the most distinctive small house in East Texas. It is double faced, the two four-columned porticoes providing entrance from either street. The interior is enhanced by paneled doors, wide windows, mellow wainscoting, and wallpaper of colonial design.

In 1903 the house was bought by the Cumberland Presbyterian Church, which used it as its manse for half a century. Now it is owned, maintained, and furnished by the Jessie Allen Wise Garden Club and serves as headquarters for the Annual Historical Pilgrimage, a project of the club, which has been held in April of each year since its inception in 1947. During the Pilgrimage the ante-bellum homes of Jefferson are opened to visitors, who are welcomed by hostesses in the costume of Jefferson's halcyon days. A parade depicts "A Pageant of Early Jefferson," and for several years there has been a stage presentation of *The Diamond Bess Murder Trial* in the Jefferson Playhouse. In 1956 the president of the sponsoring Jessie Allen Wise Garden Club was Mrs. Jack Ford.

The United States Department of the Interior has bestowed on the Old Manse a plaque marking it as "possessing exceptional historic or architectural interest."

Open to visitors during the Jefferson Pilgrimage and at other times by appointment.

Old Presbyterian Manse, built in 1839 by General James Harrison Rogers

Alley-Carlson Home

Walker and Main

DANIEL N. ALLEY, whose home is thought to be one of the four oldest in Jefferson, was a founder of the town, which is laid out on the Allen Urquhart and Daniel N. Alley additions. After the organization of Marion County in 1860, Alley offered land for the courthouse and jail, in an effort to encourage the growth of the town in the direction of the hill—in opposition to businessmen who wanted warehouses and business buildings close to the wharves of the Big Cypress. In 1869 the county accepted Alley's donation of land; and the courthouse, an interesting example of Greek Revival architecture, was completed in 1874. Its records show that later the court was directed to "re-convey" to D. N. Alley all unsold lots donated for the building of the courthouse.

The house into which the Alley family moved in 1859 is a delightful one-story cottage. The pleasant entrance porch, shading a front door with traditional side lights, has four well-proportioned Doric columns. The doors and the long, brown-shuttered windows have wide moldings. Column insets are used in the corners of the house in the old manner, and this detail is carried out in the addition, a rear wing constructed in harmony with the original house.

The interior of the house has remained much the same through the years. There are sixteen-foot ceilings, and the walls are wainscoted. The parlor contains many cherished heirlooms. A large bottle and vase collection is displayed in the house. The kitchen, now modernized, still contains many utensils of other days. Many of these rare antiques, in constant use today, were brought by river steamers from New Orleans to Jefferson.

Daniel N. Alley and his wife were proud of their daughters and built houses for them when they were married. The "bride and groom" houses standing today are the "Old Jefferson House" or W. B. Ward home, the Sedberry house or "Catalpa Villa," and the old Crawford house—all on Broadway.

The original Alley home has been continuously used as a family residence. It is now owned and occupied by Mrs. Mary Carlson, granddaughter of the family's founder. Recently the house was the scene of a reception following the ceremonies commemorating the centennial year of Jefferson's Presbyterian Church. The first property record in the history of this church was signed by Daniel N. Alley and dated July 12, 1853. On the occasion of the centennial reception his granddaughter, Mrs. Carlson, contributed a cake which was topped by a miniature replica of the church and bore one hundred candles.

Open to visitors during the Jefferson Pilgrimage and at other times by appointment.

Alley-Carlson home, occupied as a
family residence since 1859

W. B. Ward Home: "Old Jefferson House" Broadway

Sedberry House: "Catalpa Villa" Broadway

ONE OF THE ALLEY dower houses is the Colonel W. B. Ward home on Broadway. This story-and-a-half structure was built during the 1860's and presented to Virginia Alley about the time of her marriage to M. L. Crawford.

In 1876, after the untimely death of Mrs. Crawford, the house was sold to Colonel W. B. Ward. A native Texan, Colonel Ward moved to Jefferson soon after the Civil War. He became one of the town's leading businessmen and president of the Jefferson National Bank. He was also one of the promoters of the East Line–Red River Railway. From 1868 until his death in 1915—almost half a century—he was a member of the congregation of the Presbyterian Church of Jefferson. In the deed to the church property, purchased in 1871, he was a trustee signer.

The Ward home was a social and civic center for many years. The "1881 Club," the oldest chartered club in Texas, was organized here in October, 1881. A chautauqua circle was formed, composed of both men and women. Later it emerged as a woman's club, which has met continuously since its founding.

The roomy, livable house of ten rooms downstairs and three upstairs has a spacious six-columned veranda which protects the four floor-length front windows and a distinctive entrance with an ornate fan-shaped pediment. The massive portal conceals gun cabinets which open into the large front hall. The ornate panels at the entrance, the molding on the hidden gun cabinets, and the window and door facings indicate the employment of a type of plane in use before the Civil War. The stout floors and high ceilings are covered with wide hand-planed boards. In the large hall a decorated arch breaks the wide space.

Very few structural changes have been made in the house. The large back porch has been converted into a modern kitchen and bath. Sliding doors between the former front and back parlors still function. The house is now owned by Mr. and Mrs. Clarence Harland Messer and is occupied by Mr. and Mrs. A. C. Ogburn, who operate an antique shop in a portion of the residence.

AN ADAPTATION of the Louisiana "raised cottage" style is the Sedberry house, now known as "Catalpa Villa" for the enormous catalpa tree, one of the largest in America, which stands in its yard. The house combines the bricked-in bottom floor basement and raised main floor of the Louisiana style with an open first-floor hallway, or dog run, unusual in a house of more than one story, which provides an inner porch, cool in summer and private the year round.

The house, built about 1852 by slave labor, was designed and constructed by Mrs. Sedberry's father, D. N. Alley, as her wedding present. Few changes have been made in it since. The hand-hewn pine floors are still in use. The kitchen and dining room, originally downstairs, are now on the second floor. An inside stairway has been built from the brick floor of the courtyard to the living quarters on the upper floor. Latticework, banisters, and cornices are practically the same as in the early years.

Mr. and Mrs. C. A. Meisenheimer, who purchased the Sedberry home in 1933, have preserved its appearance and charm. Many beautiful antiques, including furniture, china, and silver, are to be found in the high-ceilinged rooms. A Victorian parlor suite, odd chairs, and a century-old *étagère* adorn the old parlor. A quaint drop-leaf table that is a family heirloom and an antique mirror are among other prized possessions of the owners. Many old books, magazines, and newspapers have been preserved and may be seen by visitors during the Annual Pilgrimage.

"Old Jefferson House" is open to visitors daily from 9:30 to 5; "Catalpa Villa" is open during the Jefferson Pilgrimage.

"Catalpa Villa," a dower house

"Old Jefferson House," now an antique shop

Dan Lester Home: "Guarding Oak"

Friou and Walker

A TREMENDOUS OAK TREE which stood in front of the ante-bellum home now owned and occupied by Mr. and Mrs. Dan Lester gave the house its name of "Guarding Oak." This white colonial house, in its finely landscaped green setting, is one of the most beautiful early homes to be found today in all Texas.

A near-century of use has brought many changes to this stout old structure. The original story-and-a-half home was built by A. U. Wright in 1859. Declining with the fortunes of Jefferson after the city's great days as a river port, the house was eventually converted into apartments. A fire dispossessed the tenants and badly damaged the interior of the building, but left it structurally repairable. And finally, in 1941, Mr. and Mrs. Lester restored and refinished it, bringing to light, and enhancing, its original charm.

Today the broad porch, extending across the entire front of the house, looks out over a neatly terraced lawn. The four columns, two full stories in height, that support the porch were cut from East Texas cypress. The impressive doorway, between shuttered windows, is lighted by a handsome antique porch lamp.

The large central hall affords entry into the parlor, the dining room, and three rear rooms. Each room, including the modernized kitchen, contains a fireplace. Two quaint windows fashioned with nearly a hundred panes light the sunroom. The U-shaped stairway, in the construction and restoration of which virgin timbers were used, is of exceptional architectural beauty. The floor plan of the upper story is similar to that of the lower. The space on the floor is used for three bedrooms in addition to an upstairs sitting room.

The furnishings of "Guarding Oak" are choice and beautiful. Many of the antiques to be seen in the rooms are heirlooms collected from the possessions of the pioneers of old Jefferson. In the hallway hangs a large chandelier of glass beads and hand-forged brass. Of French design, it was made in New Orleans a century ago. It was rescued from a jumbled heap in a basket and reassembled by experts.

In the drawing room are a seven-piece French Victorian suite made for a royal family, a square rosewood piano, Venetian mirrors, and elaborate lampas silk draperies, together with other furnishings of great beauty. In the dining room, beneath a massive Venetian crystal chandelier, stands a Sheraton banquet table with an inlaid border, capable of accommodating twenty guests.

Upstairs, the three bedrooms are all decorated in different styles, and all equally lovely. The Magnolia Room has solid walnut furniture, including a bed with eight-foot posts in graduated buttons which was brought to Jefferson by steamboat. One of the posts contains a secret hiding place for valuables. The French Room features an exquisite pair of Dresden and brass beds, dainty dressing tables, and colorful lamps. In the Early American Room, the massive bed is adorned with a coverlet woven in 1834.

"Guarding Oak" is one of the chief attractions of the Annual Historical Pilgrimage, of which Mrs. Lester is a leading light.

"Guarding Oak" is open to visitors during the Jefferson Pilgrimage.

"Guarding Oak," one
of Texas' most
beautiful old homes

Magnolia Room: one
of the walnut bed
posts has a hiding
place for jewels

Drawing room at
"Guarding Oak"

David Key Home: "Blue Bonnet Farm" Highway 59

Beard House Henderson and Vale

ALONG OLD TRAMMEL'S TRACE in the 1830's and 1840's a varied parade of travelers—armed bandits, hopeful settlers, curious adventurers—trekked across East Texas. Near Jefferson the Trace ran through Tuscumbia Ranch, where in 1847 Mrs. Cutrier, a widow who had brought her family and slaves from Mississippi, built a two-room cabin. Now, at what is usually called "Blue Bonnet Farm," a large and hospitable house stands on the south side of a paved highway from Marshall to Jefferson.

The transition from the original cabin to the present story-and-a-half house was gradual. First the cabin, on the side of a hill sloping to the rear, was raised and an under room was built of wood and brick. Then in 1869 the main part of the house was completed. Heart-pine, cut on the place, was used in construction throughout.

The front of the old home, as it stands now, has a porch protecting double front doors with side lights and an old iron marker. Multi-pane windows extend to the floor. The two-story ell in the rear rests on brick walls which support large rooms and an ell-shaped porch with iron banisters and stout columns. This elevated porch overlooks a bricked patio centered by a basin in the form of a Lone Star over which hovers an iron eagle, reminiscent of the old ironworks at Jefferson. A half-enclosed stairway leads from the patio to the porch and the main floor level. A long, wide hall runs from the front gallery to the back porch. Flanking it on either side are two rooms, each heated by a huge fireplace using a central flue. The rustic lower room has exposed beams, a large fireplace, and old brick walls.

Restoration of the house was begun in 1939 by Mrs. Dolly Key. Her son, David Key, and his wife, the present occupants, have completed the restoration and furnished the home with antiques appropriate to its history.

DURING THE SPRING PARADE of old homes in Jefferson's Ninth Historical Pilgrimage, the old Beard house, restored and refurnished in 1956 by Mrs. James I. Peters, was open to visitors for the first time. Often identified as the Goetzman house, the cottage was built between 1860 and 1870 by Noble A. Birge, a prominent merchant and civic leader of the day. The Birge family occupied the residence until 1874.

In the restoration of the seven-room white frame house, great care was exercised to preserve the original designs and plans. The neoclassic exterior has been meticulously restored. Glorified dentils decorate the wide cornices which extend around the entire structure. Columned porches, not identical but harmonious, shelter double doors with top lights, which provide entrance from the two streets.

The original floor plan remains intact, although a few changes have modernized the old home. The random floors, cross-paned windows, shutters, and stout hardware are still in use. The back gallery, which surrounds a stone-lined well, has been glassed in. The detached kitchen, twice moved, now functions as a garage.

The front hall leads into the living room and a front bedroom, furnished in the style of the structure's early days. The large bedroom has a carved walnut suite, a princess mirror, and a wash basin. In the parlor a handsome mirror reflects a rosewood piano inlaid with pearl. The second living room, with its large fireplace, opens on the side porch and into the glass-enclosed veranda. The dining room, bright with white wainscoting and curtains, is also furnished with period pieces.

This home has been cited by the Historical American Buildings Survey of the United States Department of the Interior as being worthy of preservation.

Both houses are open to visitors during the Jefferson Pilgrimage.

Rear view of
"Blue Bonnet Farm," home of
Mr. and Mrs. David Key

The Beard house, restored by Mrs. James I. Peters

Excelsior Hotel

Austin Street

THE NORTH PORTION of the Excelsior Hotel, which in its early days was known as the Irvine House, was built in the late 1850's by a man from New Hampshire, Captain William Perry. The captain's daughter, Lucy, is said to have been the first child born in Jefferson and the first native to be married there. Captain Perry met his death when a Yankee soldier, mistaking his identity, shot him as he stood on the corner near his home.

As Jefferson grew into its busiest years, the Irvine House expanded. In 1877 it was acquired by Mrs. Kate Wood, donor of the property on which the post office and the federal courthouse now stand. By that time the Bayou City had already angered Jay Gould by proving unreceptive to his railroad plans. At the top of a page in the hotel's register for 1872 may still be seen Gould's flourishing signature with his characteristic hasty sketch of a jaybird. At the bottom of the page he had written in pique: "The end of Jefferson."

But it was the end of neither the city nor the hotel, whose register continued to record the names of the great, even to a President of the United States. During his incumbency, President Rutherford B. Hayes, arriving on a steamer from New Orleans, was a guest of the Excelsior. In an 1878 register the signature of John Jacob Astor appears. In April, 1879, the "Ward-Barrymore Combination" with John Drew and company stayed at the hotel. In 1881 guests included W. H. Vanderbilt and General Grant, who "paid $2." Oscar Wilde, who recited poetry at the Jefferson Opera House, boarded at the Excelsior.

The present owner of the hotel, Mrs. James I. Peters, has expended much time and effort in the restoration of the building and its furnishings to the beauty they possessed in Jefferson's day of glory. The Excelsior as it is today is an ell-shaped structure. The original portion was built by Captain Perry of heavy timbers, while the newer portion is brick. The broad front veranda, set with wrought-iron benches and settees, is partially screened from the street by iron-lace work and planters of flowers. In the rear, extending the length of the two sides facing the secluded patio, is a balcony with an ornamental railing and an outside stairway from the first floor.

The patio, centered by an interesting fountain, is walled with brick. Recesses in the walls hold figurines, and decorative wrought-iron seats provide resting places along the brick walks between formal flower beds.

The bedrooms of the hotel are furnished with massive suites, marble-topped tables, quaint lamps, and old-fashioned wardrobes. One bedroom suite of carved walnut merits special attention. In the restored dining hall, an ornate Dresden chandelier hangs from the high ceiling. This room also contains several fine sideboards and serving pieces. On the broad tables are revolving silver canisters holding rare glass bottles for condiments. The mantel in the drawing room is intricately ornamented, and all the furnishings of the room carry out the elegant taste characteristic of the period.

In the comfortable lobby a square Chickering piano and several pictures lend a homelike air. A mural fashioned from wool is a collector's item. A glass showcase holds historical mementoes and records.

An old advertisement of the Irvine House appears in the directory for 1871: "Stages arrive and depart from this hotel daily." Though modes of transportation have changed, the old hotel remains to accommodate travelers and to show visitors to the Annual Historical Pilgrimage the hospitality of a more leisurely time.

Dresden chandelier in
hotel's restored dining room

Lovely Old World garden behind Excelsior Hotel

Entrance to hotel   Some of the priceless furnishings in drawing room

J. H. Scantlin House Dixon and Owens

W. P. Schluter House Line and Taylor

A CONTRAST with Jefferson's many white Greek Revival houses is furnished by the barn-red, "homespun" Scantlin home. Built in 1852 in the Alley Addition, this one-story house of Texas-Colonial frontier cottage style—formerly known as the Banta Place or Sagamore—has passed through the hands of many owners.

Gradually the old home fell into ruin. But then it was acquired by Mr. and Mrs. J. H. Scantlin, who during the past fifteen years have restored it admirably, by their own efforts with only the sporadic assistance of local hired help. Structurally, the building was still sound, as its heavy beams and wide boards are held together with wooden pegs. The original random floors and beaded ceilings are still functional and appropriate after a century of use. The moldings were rescued from the historic Governor's Mansion in Marshall when it was razed recently. Wallpapers of colonial prints are in harmony with the whole.

The cottage is fronted by a long gallery supported by four square white columns set on a reinforced brick floor. White-shuttered windows and a broad white door offer a pleasing contrast to the red of the remainder of the house. The walls of the old entrance hall have been torn away so that the entire front might be converted into a living-dining area, the conversation center of which is a massive fireplace made of old bricks and framed by carefully dried hand-planed beams. From this long room a small hall affords entrance into the modernized kitchen, the full bath, and the adjacent bedroom, all furnished in frontier style. A huge Dutch door opens from the hall onto the side veranda and down to the private flagstone-paved patio. The ell in the rear accommodates three bedrooms.

In every room of the house, Early American furnishings testify to Mrs. Scantlin's industry and taste. Rugs and curtains, her own handiwork, harmonize with the antique furniture which she has gathered and skilfully refinished. The result is a model home which attracts throngs of visitors during the Historical Pilgrimage.

A RECENT ADDITION to the list of homes to be visited in the Historical Pilgrimage is the Schluter mansion, now owned by Mr. and Mrs. J. E. Blain. Built in 1854 by the father of W. P. Schluter, this two-story frame dwelling, standing on a corner with large porches sheltering entrances from both streets, was continuously occupied by descendants of the Schluter family for almost a century.

In 1949 the Blains purchased the house from a granddaughter of the builder, and redecorated and furnished it in time for the wedding of their oldest daughter. It is now a comfortable modern dwelling, which nevertheless continues accurately to reflect the past. The imposing entrance with double doors and ornamental side lights leads into a roomy hall which is duplicated on the second floor. The lower hall with its traditional petticoat mirror and ornate stairway opens into pleasant rooms. Large rugs made from the original colonial-patterned carpeting cover the stout floors. In the drawing room decorated walnut cornices frame two windows and a French mirror. A fine chandelier lights up the elaborate Queen Anne sofa and chairs. The dining room fireplace is of Italian black marble. In the rear of the lower story are a second parlor, a convenient bedroom, and a breakfast nook.

In the front bedroom on the second floor is a walnut four-poster bed with carved spindles, together with a marble-topped dresser and chests. The one-and-a-half back settee at the foot of the bed is one of several original pieces that were brought from Natchez for a century of use in this lovely old Jefferson home.

Both houses are open during the Pilgrimage; the Scantlin home may be visited at other times by appointment, for a fee of $1.00.

(*Above*) W. P. Schluter house

(*Right*) Corner of Scantlin kitchen

(*Below, left*) Walnut cornices and French
mirror in drawing room of Schluter house

(*Below, right*) Home of Mr. and Mrs. J. H. Scantlin

Freeman Plantation House

Highway 49

STANDING HIGH on a hill five hundred feet from the highway, surrounded by a grove of ancient trees, the Freeman plantation house is located in the most beautiful natural setting of any of Jefferson's ante-bellum homes. It is readily identifiable as a Louisiana version of the Greek Revival type of home—brick basement on the ground level, ground-to-eaves pillars, and an outside stairway entering the main or upper floor. Like "Catalpa Villa," the Freeman house contains a definite Texas adaptation in the open hall, or breezeway, on the ground level behind the outside stairway.

A recorded deed dated March 15, 1850, shows the purchase of the wooded land on which the house stands by William M. Freeman for his three minor daughters. Freeman was one of the founders of the East Texas Manufacturing Company, a business designed for the "manufacture of cotton and woolen goods, spinning thread, and other fabrics for home or public use."

Reliable sources indicate that the plantation house was built in the same year in which Freeman acquired the property. Apparently no architect was required. The entire house was built by slaves who cut lumber from the virgin timber on the plantation and molded, baked, and laid the bricks. The hand-hewn beams, exposed in the brick-walled basement, that support the entire house are fourteen by fourteen inches in thickness and extend the full length of the large building. The four towering columns that uphold the roof of the suspended porch are built of brick and coated with cement.

In recent years a large wing has been added to the rear of the house to provide facilities for modern living. In the original structure the plans of the upper floor and the ground floor are identical, each having a central hall flanked by four rooms. Each of the eight rooms has a large open fireplace. The view from the attractive entrance shows the upper hall divided by a hand-carved colonnade. The large music room on the right and the drawing room on the left can be shut off by handsome folding doors which function smoothly after a century of use. Long windows on quaint balancers may still be pushed up into the attic. From the hall, which is often used as a serving area, two bedrooms may be reached, and a stairway leads to the basement. A secret panel near the landing was recently discovered, revealing some old coins and papers. Opening into the breezeway downstairs are an additional bedroom, a den, a dining room, and a kitchen with outside entrances.

During the last decade much time, effort, and money have been spent by Lawrence Flannery in the restoration and refurnishing of the Freeman house. The result has been most rewarding. Brilliant chandeliers, now wired for electricity, shine on ruby satin draperies and colonial-patterned carpets. The music room holds a square rosewood piano, carved chairs, and delicate statuary. The parlor has a quaint "chaperon sofa" and dainty serving tables. Near the end of the long hall a handsome French mirror reflects a massive banquet table. In the master bedroom stand a sturdy cherry bed and dresser that were carved by slaves. Here, also, is a large "primping sofa."

Downstairs, the den is furnished with desks, a reed organ, and a lounge. The adjoining bedroom features Early American furniture. The paneled dining room is appropriately furnished with matching maple pieces. The kitchen, now modernized, still has its open fireplace with iron kettles and pots.

The present owner of the house is Mrs. Lois Shepard. Like many other old homes of Texas, this one has been awarded the plaque of the Historic American Buildings Survey.

Open to visitors during the Jefferson Pilgrimage and at other times by appointment.

Freeman plantation house and a corner of its music room

Moores-Watts-Pryor House

1609 New Boston Road

SOMETIME DURING THE DAYS of the Texas Republic, Charles and Mary Moores came to Texas from Fairfield, South Carolina, and settled in Bowie County, in what is now Texarkana—the "Siamese twin among cities," half in Texas and half in Arkansas, with the state line running through the center of town. In the Moores family there were seven sons and five daughters. Charles Moores, one of the sons, took up land along the present Seventh Street Highway. An early-day church, known as Harrison Chapel, was founded on this spot. Though the church is now gone, the old family cemetery may still be seen.

When another son, Eli Harrison Moores, married Minerva A. Janes in 1847, his father deeded to him as a nuptial gift a large tract of land "in consideration of natural affection." The first house built on the property was a log cabin. Later a larger and more pretentious structure was erected in front of the cabin. The new one-story home followed the current plan of building, a center hallway with rooms to either side. In this instance, the milk shed at the back of the house was connected with the long hallway.

Some years later another tract of land was given Eli Moores, and by his own industry and thrift he also acquired property in the downtown section of Texarkana. Moores was esteemed for his generosity: he gave the original building sites for the First Baptist Church, the Presbyterian Church, and the Sacred Heart Church.

During the Mexican War, some one thousand troops under the command of John P. Gaines camped on the Moores property. These were soldiers who had been recruited in Kentucky and were en route to Mexico.

Eli and Minerva Moores were the parents of four sons and four daughters. The old home place, with the surrounding property, was inherited by a daughter, Nannie Moores. In 1894 she married

John C. Watts, and to this union eight children were born. One of these, a daughter, Mrs. Judson Pryor, owns the home today and resides there with her family.

The Moores home has been extensively remodeled twice, once in the 1890's and again during the past decade. It is now a modern two-story dwelling in a lovely setting of shrubs and trees. The center hallway remains unchanged except for the addition of a broad stairway built when the second story was added. The rooms to one side, originally a small living room and two bedrooms, have been made into a single large living room running the length of the house. On the other side of the central entrance way, the rooms once used as bedroom and kitchen have now been combined to form a dining room, while an addition at the rear contains the kitchen. In the present arrangement, the upper story provides space for bedrooms and baths.

Antique furniture may be seen throughout the house. The living room has a lovely Victorian sofa and chair set, and marble-topped tables, mirrors, and silver are additional reminders of years gone by.

In 1947 a centennial tea for two thousand guests was given to celebrate the hundredth anniversary of the original gift of the homesite, the deed for which was exhibited at the tea. The old smokehouse, now used as a summerhouse, sheltered the orchestra during the festivities. Refreshments were served from an ice punch bowl which bore the date 1847 outlined in flowers frozen in the ice. Thus fittingly was celebrated the end of a century during which three generations of the Moores-Watts-Pryor families had lived in this substantial Texarkana landmark.

The Pryor home is not open to visitors.

Home of Mrs. Judson Pryor, granddaughter of the original owner

Charles DeMorse House Comanche Street, Clarksville

Collin McKinney House Finch Park, McKinney

RED RIVER COUNTY, of which Clarksville is the county seat, has some claim to the title of "mother county of Texas," since—through a misunderstanding as to which river was the international boundary at that point—it was colonized some years before Austin's settlement at San Felipe. Among those for whom it was the gateway to Texas were Sam Houston and David Crockett.

James Clark, the pioneer who gave Clarksville its name, persuaded Isaac Smathers and his family to settle in the new town, offering as inducement a block of land and help on his new house. Smathers accepted the offer, and the house was erected the next day by a community "log raising." This house, built in 1833, later became the nucleus of the home of Colonel Charles DeMorse, the "Father of Texas Journalism."

DeMorse came to Texas at the age of twenty, hoping to take part in the struggle for independence. Arriving just too late to fight in the Battle of San Jacinto, he began to practice law in Matagorda, where he met and married Miss Lodiska Wooldridge. In 1842 he was invited by Red River District representatives to the Texas Congress, for which he had edited a weekly periodical, to establish a newspaper in Clarksville.

The *Northern Standard* began publication on August 20, 1842. A log house first served as the paper's office, but in 1855 a brick building was erected near the editor's home. This building, said to be one of the first brick structures in northeast Texas, was demolished in 1927. It had housed the pioneer publication under DeMorse and his daughter, Mrs. Isabelle DeMorse Latimer, for nearly fifty years. The *Standard* ceased publication in 1887, the year of DeMorse's death.

In 1842 DeMorse enlarged and remodeled his home. Using hand-hewn lumber, he added seven new rooms to the original two. The furnishings included built-in bookcases, a fine clock which still tells time, and a piano which was shipped from New York to Jefferson by water and thence to Clarksville by oxcart. Among many pieces of period furniture, the editor's desk with its inkwells and files is particularly noteworthy.

Three generations have lived in the Charles DeMorse homestead. A granddaughter, Miss Isabelle Latimer, now occupies the house, in the front yard of which stands a Centennial marker, erected in 1936, honoring the pioneer journalist.

IN FINCH PARK in McKinney is the home of Collin McKinney, constructed in 1832. Originally it stood some seventeen miles north of the present town, but as a part of the 1936 Centennial celebration it was moved to a more convenient location, a gift of the McKinney heirs to the city. Later it was placed in Finch Park.

Collin McKinney, a Kentuckian by birth, was one of the five committeemen who composed the Texas Declaration of Independence, as well as one of the fifty-nine signers of that document. He represented his community in the first four Congresses of the Republic. Before he died in 1861 at the age of ninety-five the Texas patriot had lived under eight flags: British Colonial, Thirteen Colonies, Spanish, Mexican, Texas Provisional, Texas Republic, United States, and Confederate.

The McKinney home is a story-and-a-half log house with an attic and a wide stone fireplace. Recently the McKinney Garden Club raised funds to repair the house, now a public museum. Suitable old lumber was used for siding. The chimney was rebuilt with native stone, and the old hearth was reproduced to accommodate an iron crane and pot. Other items of interest include a showcase for records and papers, ironstone dishes, and hand-woven materials. The museum is supervised by the custodian of Finch Park.

The DeMorse house is not open to visitors; the McKinney house may be seen by appointment with the park custodian.

Collin McKinney house, built in 1832

Charles DeMorse homestead, part of it built in 1833 by a community "log raising"

Captain Rawlins House Highway 342, Lancaster

Overton House 3550 Overton Road, Honey Springs

THE CAPTAIN RAWLINS HOUSE was built by the son of the earliest settler of the Lancaster area. Roderick Rawlins moved to Texas from Illinois in 1844 with his family and took up headrights on the present site of Lancaster, where he lived until his death in 1848.

His son Roderick A. Rawlins was eight years old when he arrived in Texas with the family. He attended the first school of the area, and later in his school career he was taught by Miss Virginia Bledsoe, whose father, A. Bledsoe, bought half of the Rawlins headright and there laid out, in 1847, the town of Lancaster.

After some time young Rawlins married his teacher, who was only one year his senior. He and his bride built and occupied the Rawlins home in 1857. The timbers for the house, cut from trees along Ten Mile Creek, were prepared with a broadax and an adz brought on the long trek to Texas. The flooring and siding were sawed lumber from two mills in the Trinity River bottoms. At first the house consisted of a large room with two doors and four windows, a half-story above, and a lean-to divided into two rooms for bedroom and kitchen. A stairway led from the kitchen to the attic. Near by were the dug well, the smokehouse, a corn bin, and orchards.

When Captain Rawlins returned from service with the Confederate army he found his house dilapidated. But he set to work to repair and enlarge it, securing money and materials by trade in farm products. Finally the original house became a spacious home of eleven rooms. The dog-run between two earlier portions was turned into a hall with double doors, lighted by top panes. Three gables were set into the roof in front. End chimneys furnished heat.

At present Erle Rawlins, Jr., a direct descendant cf the builder, and his two brothers, R. A. Rawlins and F. M. Rawlins, are restoring the old home for use as a week-end house for the family.

REPUTEDLY the first frame house built in Dallas County, the William Perry Overton home was started in 1853 and completed the following year. The builder was the ninth child of Aaron Overton, and came with his father to Texas in 1844, when the elder Overton became the seventh actual settler in Dallas County. The father and two sons who had accompanied him—the other was C. C. Overton—raised a log cabin, cleared land near a small creek, and built a flour mill at the foot of the hill on their Honey Springs headright. The mill, first of its kind in the county, had a capacity of a hundred bushels of wheat daily. In 1847 Aaron Overton made the long trip back to Missouri and brought the rest of his family to Honey Springs.

William Perry Overton took up a headright adjoining that of his father, built a small cabin, and devoted himself to farming and milling. In 1847 he married Miss Martha Ann Newton of Missouri. In 1853 he traded his headright to his father for the elder Overton's interests at Honey Springs. He then continued in the milling business until 1866, when he returned to farming.

The timber that was fashioned into the William Overton dwelling was hauled from Palestine in Anderson County. The house was built in an oak grove, some of the trees in which were felled to a level and used as supports under the building. The two-story house has a double porch across the front and one end. The massive chimneys at each end of the front portion still rest on their original bases of native stone. The wing at the back of the house is connected with the front hall and is divided into several large rooms.

Ruby E. Overton now lives in the ancestral home. Other descendants of the pioneering Overtons live near by. After a century of use, the old landmark is in a good state of preservation.

Neither house is open to visitors.

Captain Roderick A. Rawlins house,
owned by three generations
of Rawlinses

William Perry Overton house, reputedly the first frame house in Dallas County

John Neely Bryan Cabin

Courthouse Lawn

ON THE LAWN of the Dallas County courthouse now stands the reconstructed log cabin of John Neely Bryan, the first citizen of Dallas. Small among the skyscrapers of the modern city, the one-room log hut with its clay-chinked chimney is a sturdy reminder of pioneering in Dallas.

In 1840 young John Neely Bryan of Tennessee prospected on his horse, Walking Wolf, along the banks of the Trinity River. Within the limits of the Peters Colony Bryan camped on the river bank, where in November, 1841, he erected a pole tent. Except for an occasional stranger, Bryan was alone with his horse and his bear dog, Tubby, till the spring of 1842. Then several families came from Bird's Fort, a Ranger stockade, to settle in the Trinity basin. The family of Captain Gilbert left the fort in a canoe, and that of John Beeman by ox wagon, and both settled near Bryan's hut. Finally John Neely Bryan secured as his headright from the Republic of Texas a section, 640 acres of land, fronting on the Trinity where a part of Dallas now stands.

In 1842 young Bryan married John Beeman's daughter Margaret, at Fort Bonham. The two returned on ponies to the log cabin which Bryan had already built. After it was destroyed by a flood the following year, he built a second log cabin, the one which is now, in reconstructed form, on the courthouse lawn, near its original site.

The cabin is built of native twelve-inch hewn-cedar logs, chinked with clay. The only door, at the front, is made of heavy boards and fastened with a latchstring. The two windows, both protected by heavy wooden shutters, hang on hand-wrought hinges. The roof, the only part of the cabin not in the original hut, is made of rived shingles representative of those used in roofs of Bryan's day. A puncheon floor of flat cedar logs and a limestone fireplace were fashioned by the pioneer owner.

Having modified his original plans for a trad-ing post, Bryan founded a town on his land. He used his cabin for a store, carrying a stock of powder, whiskey, tobacco, piece goods, and small tools. In a borrowed wagon he hauled trinkets for the store over his trail, now Preston Road. The first church services were probably held in the cabin. There, too, Bryan served the community as its first lawyer. He also operated the first ferry across the Trinity, in the early 1840's.

According to many reports and records, the Bryan cabin gradually became a community center for the Trinity area. In 1846 the environs of the cabin were surveyed and platted for a town, in accordance with an act of the Texas legislature. The village was named Dallas, reputedly for George M. Dallas, Vice-President of the United States under President Polk. In 1850, in a spirited election, Dallas was chosen as the county seat over Hord's Ridge, now Oak Cliff. From 1848 to 1850 the Bryan home was used as a courthouse.

In 1852 Bryan sold his holdings to Alexander Cockrell for $7,000. He then left his family in Dallas and joined the gold rush to California. He returned to Dallas eventually, and spent his declining years in Texas.

For many years the Bryan cabin was neglected and almost forgotten. It was finally removed from its second site at Buckner's Orphans Home to its present location. In 1936 it was restored under the auspices of the Dallas Historical Society and the Commissioners Court of Dallas County, and opened to the public as a memorial museum. Later a shelter was erected over the small hut. John Neely Bryan's legacy, found in the cabin, consists of a built-in bed, fastened to the wall, and a picture of himself and his wife.

Open to visitors Monday through Friday, 9:30 a.m. to 4:30 p.m.; Saturdays, 9:30 a.m. to 12 noon.

Reconstructed log cabin of John Neely Bryan, first citizen of Dallas

Judge William H. Hord House

Marsalis Park

ON A HIGH BLUFF overlooking Cedar Creek, among oak and walnut trees on the edge of a wilderness, William H. Hord built his home in 1845. Just a few months before, his wife, three sons, and three Negro servants had accompanied him on the long trek in covered wagons from Tennessee to the Trinity River. The entire family worked at the new venture of setting up a homestead in the virgin country. Since it was on the west bank of the Trinity, the new headright of the Hords lay in Robertson County. William Hord laid off his farm, a mile square, on a ridge east of the present Beckley Road. His headright covered part of what is now the business section of Oak Cliff.

The Hord home grew with the family. The two older boys and Uncle Bruin, a Negro slave, helped with broadaxes and frows to fell big cedars and hew logs for the first room, twenty by twenty-five feet. They fashioned a puncheon floor of oak and built white stones into a chimney. As time went on the house developed in typical Texas style, so that eventually it had a closed dog-run hall flanked by two large rooms, with a veranda across the front. A lean-to on the rear provided more room for the family of eight children.

The Hord farmstead became the center about which grew Hord's Ridge, a competitor with the village of Dallas on the opposite bank of the Trinity. In 1850 the two, together with Cedar Springs, were rivals for the title of county seat of Dallas County, which had been organized from Nacogdoches and Robertson counties. Hord's Ridge was favored because of the lack of ferries across the Trinity and the impassable river bottoms. But after Cedar Springs had been eliminated, Dallas defeated Hord's Ridge by a vote of 244 to 216 and became the county seat.

From 1848 to 1850 Judge Hord served as the second judge of Dallas County. It was he who married the first couple in the county after it was organized. In 1860 the Hord home escaped destruction in the big Dallas fire, and Judge Hord helped to restore order in the town when sentiment ran high against Negroes and abolitionists who were accused of causing the conflagration. The judge and his posse broke up a crowd of angry citizens who had congregated at the east ferry landing to lynch some unfortunate Negroes. During the Civil War, Judge Hord and three of his sons served in the Confederate army. One son was killed on the battlefield, but the others returned to the Hord plantation after the war.

With the turn of the century, the old landmark fell into decay; but it was finally restored and incorporated in Marsalis Park. The present structure, though enlarged for use as a recreation hall, contains all the original materials of the old homestead. It was made usable and attractive by Mr. and Mrs. Martin Weiss of Dallas. Martin Weiss, upon becoming president of the Oak Cliff Commercial Association, later known as the Oak Cliff Chamber of Commerce, helped form American Legion Post No. 275. In 1926 he bought the Hord place, which he and Mrs. Weiss restored, and turned it over to the Post. The Post honored them by renaming the old homestead the Weiss Memorial Park.

Standing on its original site, the Hord-Weiss Memorial Home overlooks the park and zoo on old Cedar Creek. It is situated three miles from the Dallas courthouse on the Lancaster Road, at the entrance to Marsalis Park. Though it houses the Oak Cliff American Legion, the house is also used as a community center and a gathering place for many organizations.

Open to visitors by request.

The Hord house, restored and presented by Mr. and Mrs. Martin Weiss to American Legion Post No. 275 for a recreation hall and community center

Barry Miller Home: "Millermore"

3110 Bonnie View Road

ALL OF NORTH TEXAS was a vast wilderness, and Dallas was only a cluster of log cabins on the Trinity River, when William B. Miller, prospector from Kentucky, Alabama, and Missouri, came to the new town in the early 1840's. He took up a headright of 640 acres a few miles from the settlement in Precinct No. 1 of Dallas County. Then he headed back to Missouri to bring his family and his slaves to their new land in Texas. Like most pioneers, the Millers came in wagons along the trails that led to the Trinity.

During their first Texas years, the Millers lived in a sturdy log cabin with one large room, heated by a chimney of native stone, and an attic above. Built in 1847 of hand-hewn oak and cedar logs with wrought-iron nails, it stands today near the more recent Miller home as one of the oldest structures in Dallas County. The original chimney is no longer there: it was destroyed by a storm in 1899 and was rebuilt. Also missing is a wing on the north side which was used as the first boarding school for young ladies in Dallas County and its environs. The original old cedar stairs, used by the girls to climb into their room in the attic, remain in the stout old building, as do the original doors. Gone from the east side of the cabin, however, is the wide veranda, some twenty feet long, where Mr. Miller liked to sit and eat peaches from his own orchard. A spring house, built over a live spring that never ran dry, vanished long ago.

William Miller's interests were varied. In 1847 he installed a ferry across the Trinity River, which gave the people of the Hutchins community a better and more convenient approach to Dallas than they had had by way of the old Lancaster Road. In due time he enlarged his holdings by buying land, operating a flour mill, and farming. In his capacity as farmer he raised good stock and fine fruits.

In 1855 William Miller chose a hillock on his broad acres overlooking the village of Dallas as the site for a new home. He secured a tract of 1,280 acres, which had been patented by the state to a Mr. Van Cleve, for $1.00 per acre. The rapid increase of values is shown by the fact that Miller later sold seventy acres of his farm land for $30.00 per acre, and then in a repurchase paid $1,250 for two acres.

The comfortable Southern Colonial house Miller built was patterned after those left behind in the old states. Pegging the floor at night so that he could use the North Star as a compass, he faced the house due south to catch any breeze. Huge cedars and oaks were felled by his slaves on his own land and dragged by oxen to the high site. Oxen also pulled wagonloads of cypress lumber from Jefferson. The heavy timbers were fitted together by handmade wooden pins and hand-wrought iron nails. Native stone from Mountain Creek was used for the massive chimneys and hearths.

When the house was finished, nine rooms, each twenty feet square, clustered around wide cross-halls. The front porch, with its row of tall Greek columns, measured forty-seven feet in length. The ell-shaped wing at the rear was shaded by porches which sheltered an underground cistern. (This is still in use, with its windlass and bucket hanging on cedar beams.) The original kitchen was outside, between the main house and the slave cabins.

"Millermore," as this fine home is appropriately called, remains after a century on the crest of the lawn left from the original homestead. Very few changes have been made in the well-preserved house. The plaster on the handmade oak laths is still strong and smooth. The floors of hand-hewn oak are polished and bright. The front hall floor has been re-covered with cedar from the puncheon floor of the old Miller cabin, matching the solid cedar stairway and railing.

"Millermore" is still the Miller family home. Its first mistress, Mrs. Emma Dewey Miller, equipped the house with substantial furnishings

(Left) Typical of "Millermore's" furnishings; *(right)* original home of William Miller

"Millermore," as it stands today — built in 1855

from the Old South. Following her lead, various members of the family have kept the home and its furnishings in good condition. Much of the original fine furniture is still in use. Marble-top tables, old cherry desks, samplers, and other relics are museum pieces. The library, which was once the family sitting room, contains about three thousand volumes. The adjacent trophy room is full of early Texana.

William B. Miller's daughter, Minnie, married Barry Miller, later lieutenant-governor of Texas. "Millermore" became their home and the center of many social affairs. Mrs. Barry Miller and her daughter, Mrs. Evelyn Miller Crowell, still continue the hospitable and gracious traditions of "Millermore" on Bonnie View Road.

Open to visitors on written request.

Rio Grande and
Southeast Texas

Viceregal Palace

Off Highway 80

THE OLDEST HOUSE in Texas, according to various records, is the viceregal palace at San Elizario in El Paso County. It was built in 1683 by the Spanish viceroy, Don Juan de Castañeda, to be used as his residence, presidio, and court of justice for the administration of the first civil settlement of Spaniards in the upper Rio Grande Valley. Near it is the site to which the mission church of San Elzeario (the spelling used on the historical marker at the site) was moved in 1773 from what is now Ciudad Juarez, Mexico.

Originally the palace stood at one corner of a ten-acre plot of land which was surrounded by a high adobe wall. The twelve-room Spanish mansion was built of sun-baked adobe brick, made by Indian slaves from native clay and straw. A surfacing of plaster on both exterior and interior protected the adobe. The walls of the structure were thirty inches thick, and the door facings were slanted to facilitate passage. The ceilings, fastened to a flat roof, were fifteen feet high and were decorated with figures of angels, a motif common in the Spanish architecture of that period.

The throne room, which is unusually large, is of special interest because of the tree painted on the north wall and the painted wainscoting that simulates a log fence. According to legend the tree was painted there because all the civil courts of the king of Spain, to be legal, had to be conducted under the boughs of a tree. No trees being available in the semiarid region of San Elizario, the towering tree was painted on the wall and ceiling over the throne of justice, with the wainscoting beneath it made to resemble an outdoor enclosure, so that at least the letter of the law might be carried out.

In addition to the main building, the viceregal establishment included quarters for the Indian slaves; barns, granaries, a mill, and storage bins; stables and lots for the horses belonging to the official family; and a well which supplied the mansion with good water and also furnished water for the imported shrubs and plants in the garden.

The little town of San Elizario has had a dramatic history since the viceregal palace was built there. The Spanish rule was overthrown by Mexican insurgents. Then the Texans forced the Mexicans to evacuate their stronghold in the palace and raised the flag of the Republic of Texas over its walls. In 1849 American troops were garrisoned in the town for a short time. From 1856 until the beginning of the Civil War the Jeff Davis camel caravans passed through its streets en route from the Gulf to Arizona. Then the Confederate flag flew above the old adobe walls until, in 1862, the California Volunteers raised the Union flag in its stead. And even after the Civil War there was violence in San Elizario when, during the Salt War in 1877, Judge Charles H. Howard, his agent, and a merchant, who had taken refuge in the viceregal mansion from a band of Mexicans bent on vengeance for the Judge's monopoly of the salt from salt lakes near by, were captured and shot.

After that the history of the old Spanish colonial landmark became more serene. For many years it was owned by a family named Ellis. Soon after the turn of the century it was bought by Judge Leigh Clark of El Paso. Judge Clark and his wife restored and maintained the historic building; but after the judge's death Mrs. Clark found herself unable to carry the burden alone, and in 1943 she sold the historic estate. Today the owner is Frank A. Smith of Clint, Texas. Of the original twelve rooms, only the Justice Chamber and three other rooms remain, in a long building which is in fair condition for tenant occupancy.

The Viceregal Palace, built in 1683, during the
Spanish occupation of Texas

Charles Stillman House

1305 Washington

ON A BUSY STREET in the business district of Brownsville stands the home of the city's founder, Charles Stillman, built for his bride in 1850. The one-story house with its end chimneys, its large front porch, its row of heavy columns, and its shuttered windows shows a combination of Mexican and southern influences. The front door, decorated with top and side lights, leads into a wide central hall. The comfortable house is still in good condition after more than a century of use.

Charles Stillman was the son of a Yankee seafarer, Captain Francis Stillman, who acquired a large fleet of sailing vessels which traded in many ports. In 1840 the Captain sailed into the mouth of the Rio Grande, seeking new trade centers. So successful was his initial venture that he rerouted most of his ships for sailing in Mexican waters. He established a large warehouse at Matamoros, on the Mexican side of the Rio Grande, and made his son Charles the manager of the new business.

On May 9, 1846, United States troops under General Zachary Taylor defeated the Mexican army under General Mariana Arista at the Battle of Resaca de la Palma, thus securing Texas' claim to the territory between the Nueces and the Rio Grande. The next year Charles Stillman bought the site of old Fort Brown and some adjacent lands across the river from Matamoros, with a view to establishing a town there. In 1848 he hired George Lyons of New Orleans to map out the proposed town of Brownsville. Stillman named the main street Elizabeth for his fiancée, Elizabeth Pamela Goodrich, whom he married the following year. He named St. Francis Street for his father and St. Charles Street for himself. Brownsville stands on historic ground, near the site of the first European settlement in Cameron County—"Rancho Viejo," established in 1771 by José Salvador de la Garza.

After the Mexican War the Stillmans went into business with Captains Richard King and Mifflin

Kenedy to buy the steamboats which General Taylor had used to transport his troops and supplies across the Rio Grande. The partners opened the Rio Grande to navigation, and for two decades controlled much of the commerce of northern Mexico. The growth of trade thus stimulated also played a large part in the development of Brownsville and the Rio Grande Valley on the United States side of the river.

Stillman's faith in the destiny of Brownsville was great. When the Federal troops left Brownsville in 1859, he wrote: "What has induced our government to withdraw their forces from this place is difficult for me to divine, for it is the most important point in Texas." Wars and blockades failed to shake his faith. Finally peace came to Brownsville when the last battle of the Civil War was fought near by, at Palmito Ranch, on May 13, 1865—thirty-four days after General Lee had surrendered at Appomattox. The Confederates won the belated battle, heard from their prisoners the outcome of the war, and surrendered to their Union captives.

Only his advancing years and his wife's determination to rear their family in the North uprooted Charles Stillman in 1866 from the Texas that he loved. His son James Stillman—one of six children, of whom three were born in Brownsville—became president of the National City Bank of New York and later chairman of its board.

The present occupant of the Stillman house, A. Trevino, is a descendant of the family who bought the place from Charles Stillman many years ago. In 1936 a Centennial marker was erected in front of the old home. And in March, 1955, it was the focal point of the welcome given members of the Stillman and Rockefeller families when they visited Brownsville and participated, with other notables, in the presentation of handsome portraits of Charles and Elizabeth Stillman at the Fort Brown Memorial Center.

Home of Charles Stillman, founder of Brownsville

George Evans House: "Centennial House"

411 North Broadway

THE FIRST two-story house built in Corpus Christi, it is said, and also the first to include a cellar, was what is now popularly called the Evans house. Built in 1848 or 1849, it has after more than a century the additional distinction of being reputedly the oldest house still standing in the city.

The builder of the pioneer house was Captain Forbes Britton, who traveled to Texas with his family from Mississippi. Perhaps he may have been persuaded to choose Corpus Christi as his destination by some of the publicity issued by Colonel Henry L. Kinney, who settled in the area in 1839 and became an effective early-day real estate promoter. The town was originally Kinney's Trading Post, or Kinney's Ranch. But in his campaign to secure more settlers Kinney adopted for the town the name Corpus Christi—which had been given to the bay by an early Spanish explorer —"as something more definite, for a postmark on the letters was needed."

Whether or not Captain Britton had heard Kinney's enthusiastic praise of "the Italy of America," he decided to build his home there. He built solidly, for the walls of the house are eighteen inches thick. They are fashioned of shell, concrete, and brick. Early-day craftsmen in search of local building materials ground oyster shell and combined it with sand and chemical additives to form a shell brick which was widely used in the Corpus Christi area.

The house stands today with minor alterations. A one-story wing has replaced an earlier two-story ell. The circular staircase in the large hallway has been removed. Recently, when a part of a one-story wing was being repaired, heavy timbers of very odd sizes were revealed. Some builders believe that these were originally brought to Corpus Christi for use in shipbuilding, since no native timbers of this description were available when the house was built and since the timbers were of sizes and lengths unheard of for house construction.

The Evans house has had many owners and occupants. In the 1850's Morris Levy of New Orleans purchased the property. A little later it was bought by a man named Howell, who is said to have left the place in the hands of a Negro servant for the duration of the Civil War. When Federal soldiers entered Corpus Christi they took over the building for their own use. The cellar became a kitchen and officers' mess hall, the remainder of the house a hospital.

Judge Pat O. Docharty, James and Janet Bryden, Mrs. Oscar Staples, and George Evans were other owners of the old residence. Evans came into possession of it in 1880. A Bostonian by birth, he arrived in Corpus Christi as a very young man and there married Cornelia Moore, daughter of a veteran of the Civil War, a distinguished South Texas settler. Evans was mayor of Corpus Christi in the 1880's. He and his descendants remained owners of the house for fifty-six years.

Since 1936 the historic landmark has been owned and maintained by Southern Minerals Corporation. The firm has used great care in preserving the dwelling's fundamental characteristics of dignity and spaciousness, and has endeavored to reproduce its original appearance.

The Evans house was renamed "Centennial House" in 1949 during the celebration of its hundredth birthday. To commemorate this event a plaque was placed in the front yard. It reads:

Centennial House has figured prominently in local, as well as state and national history. She has housed many great men and withstood wars, epidemic, hurricane and flood. She stands as a sentinel of the bluff, a monument to the stout-hearted people who built our country and made it great.

Open to visitors by appointment.

"Centennial House," oldest house in Corpus Christi

McGloin House

1½ miles southeast

PROBABLY THE ONLY DWELLING of a Texas empresario which remains standing today is the home of James McGloin, built in 1855 near San Patricio. The white frame cottage is Texan in style, with the typical front porch, end chimneys, and central hall of the pioneer house.

In 1828 McGloin and his partner, John McMullen, secured from the Mexican government a grant of land for the settlement of two hundred families. In July, 1829, the empresarios engaged two ships to carry their colonists from New York to Texas. Most of the settlers traveled at their own expense. They landed in 1830 at El Copano, at that time an important Texas port, twelve miles southeast of Refugio.

McMullen and McGloin named their Irish colony for its patron saint, San Patricio de Hibernia, St. Patrick of Ireland. The town of San Patricio, seat of the colony, was laid out four years after the landing of the settlers. It was located some distance inland, for the Mexican government allowed no settlements within twenty-five miles of the coast, the coastal strip being reserved for government control of customs, shipping, and ports.

The new town soon figured in the Texas fight for independence. On October 9, 1835, Colonel Ben Milam and James Collinsworth, with fifty volunteers, stormed the Mexican garrison at Goliad. The surprise attack was successful, the Texans capturing the entire garrison and a valuable store of supplies. Encouraged, the Texans began preparations to attack Lipantitlan, near San Patricio. The Mexicans there asked McGloin for the use of the cannon which was at San Patricio, saying it was just to "exercise the men." McGloin refused, on the ground that the cannon was not his personal property but belonged to the settlers. The Mexicans then enlisted the aid of the Ayuntamiento, or Council, which handed the cannon over to them.

Incensed by this action, the Texans determined to capture the Mexican force. When they attacked the camp, the Mexican officers and some eighty men were out hunting. The garrison surrendered without so much as firing one shot; but the other force, angry at having been caught off guard, vowed to retake the place. A pitched battle followed in which several Mexicans were killed. The only Texan casualty was the loss of three fingers by one soldier.

The next episode was not, however, so successful for the Texas cause. An expedition against Matamoros was authorized by the Texas provisional council. It was to be headed by Colonel J. W. Fannin, Colonel Francis W. Johnson, and Dr. James Grant. While the main body of troops was at Goliad, some fifty were at San Patricio under Colonel Johnson. The Mexican commander, Colonel Urrea, assembled an impressive force of three hundred cavalry and six hundred infantry. On February 17, 1836, this army started toward San Patricio; and on February 27, in a surprise move, they attacked Colonel Johnson's small force. All except Johnson and four others were killed or captured. Urrea then set out to destroy a small force under Dr. Grant which was rounding up horses for Fannin's cavalry along the Nueces River near Agua Dulce. While the Texas Declaration of Independence was being adopted at Washington-on-the-Brazos, Urrea massacred most of Grant's men some twenty miles from San Patricio.

The later history of San Patricio was more peaceful. But after its founder, James McGloin, had built his home there, he did not live long to enjoy it. He died in 1856, only one year after the house was built. Now the old home, which was recently restored, is maintained as a dwelling on the McGloin estate. The property is owned by Roger B. McGloin, a direct descendant of the empresario.

Open to visitors daily.

Two views of the James McGloin house,
probably the only Texas empresario's
home standing today

William H. Boyd House 203 West Market
Captain Barton Peck House Off Highway 59

THE NAME OF GOLIAD, the town in whose life the Boyd house now takes a vital part by housing the public library, rings heroically in Texas history. "Remember the Alamo! Remember Goliad!" was the cry with which the Texans charged at the Battle of San Jacinto. It was a call for vengeance for the massacre of Palm Sunday, March 27, 1836, in which the Mexicans murdered more than three hundred Texan prisoners at the presidio at Goliad.

Some twenty years after the massacre, during the early statehood of Texas, the Boyd house was built. In 1846-47 a stonemason and contractor named McHugh reputedly did much building in the area, where hard limestone was quarried. With this and other native materials McHugh built the two-story Boyd house, one of the oldest homes in Goliad. The limestone walls were fifteen inches thick. Pine lumber was used throughout, and the beams were unusually heavy by today's standards. Repairs to the ground floor have revealed substantial random flooring. Originally, an outside stairway led to a second-floor opening in the middle of the south wall.

Before 1863, the building was used as a drugstore and as a print shop. Then William H. Boyd rented the place, which he later bought, to accommodate his large family. An inside stairway and several partitions were erected to make living quarters consisting of four bedrooms on the second floor and a living room and parlor on the ground floor. The house was heated by a single huge fireplace on each floor. The kitchen, dining room, and cistern gallery were set apart.

Boyd first bought the property at public auction during the Civil War, when the former owner, David Taylor, was declared an "enemy alien" and his holdings were confiscated for the benefit of Confederate financing. After the war, in 1867, Taylor claimed and recovered the property. Boyd then paid for it again and secured a second deed.

Members of the Boyd family lived in the old home until 1945. Then a granddaughter, Suella Boyd Starr, sold the place to Mrs. Ida Parks Huggins to be used as a library, a memorial to her pioneer parents, Mr. and Mrs. Sol Parks. Mrs. Huggins presented the property to Goliad County, and since that time the Parks Memorial Library has proved its great value to the town of Goliad.

JUST TOO LATE to join Texas' fight for freedom, for which he had raised a volunteer regiment in Indiana, Captain Barton Peck arrived in Texas in 1836 and found that this was the place where he wanted to make his home. He met and married a native Texan, Frances O. Menefee, and in 1842 he built his house on a hill west of Goliad.

The two-story dwelling, constructed of native stone and stucco, has tall columns supporting an entrance porch and its balcony and protecting the imposing doorways. The central halls for the lower and upper levels, lighted by decorative panes above the front doors, provide access to spacious rooms. The substantial home has needed few changes and only minor repairs.

Among the interesting furnishings is a rosewood desk made from a square piano which was the property of Captain Peck. A secretary which once belonged to a state senator is still in constant use. Tall canopied beds, large wardrobes, and the inevitable washstands make up the essentially Texas Colonial bedroom furnishings.

The house has always belonged to members of the Peck family. Sue Peck, daughter of Captain Barton Peck, married Judge J. Guy Patton in 1867. The Pattons bought the interests of the other heirs. When the elder Pattons died, the old Peck home became the property of their daughter, Mrs. John Von Dohlen, who now resides there with her family.

The Boyd house is open to visitors daily from 3 p.m. to 5 p.m.; the Peck house from 3 p.m. to 4 p.m.

(Above) William H. Boyd house, with limestone walls fifteen inches thick

(Left) Captain Barton Peck house, owned by the Peck family since 1842

(Below) Side view of Peck house

William L. Callender House

1505 North Moody

THOUGH THERE IS some controversy about the matter, the Callender house is thought to be the first precut house ever built in Texas. One newspaper account states that the house was built of pine and oak shipped by boat from New York. A second version, however, has it that the lumber was cut in Florida and hauled overland to the building site. The present occupant of the house, Mrs. Eloise Callender Watson—granddaughter of William L. Callender, prominent attorney, who bought the home in 1871 and occupied it until his death in 1895—supports this version.

The house was planned in 1854 by Dr. Stephen F. Cocke, an early pastor of the First Presbyterian Church. The lumber was intended for the construction of a hunting lodge on the San Antonio River; and Mrs. Watson recalls tales that the lodge was actually erected, then taken down in numbered pieces and re-erected at the present location. In any event, Dr. Cocke died after the material arrived in Victoria, and his brother, Dr. Thomas R. Cocke, used the lumber to build a home for his niece, Mrs. J. M. Cochran.

Thomas Cocke, a Kentuckian, had traveled to Arkansas in 1844 and there had met and joined a group of nine men who were planning a trip to Texas. Victor M. Rose, in his history of Victoria County published in 1883, describes their trip and the town of Victoria as they found it:

They were forced to camp out every night of the long journey, there being no houses of accommodation the greater part of the way. The city of Victoria at that period possessed but few attractions other than those bequeathed by nature. There were but two or three brick chimneys in the town, and but one or two respectable frame buildings. The majority of the houses were made of split puncheons and round poles, the crevices daubed with mud and moss; nor were they arranged in any particular order.

Dr. Cocke established his home on the Guadalupe River and returned to bring his family to the new country. He was placed in charge of the military hospital which received patients en route to the Mexican War. In 1848 Dr. Daniel Baker ordained him as an elder in the Presbyterian church. Several years later he was elected to the state legislature, where he served with distinction.

The age of the house which Dr. Cocke built for his niece was established some years ago, when Mrs. Lloyd M. Stevens, daughter of William L. Callender and half-sister to Mrs. Eloise Callender Watson's father, found in one of the hand-hewn oak window casings a Presbyterian paper bearing the date of 1857 and containing the inaugural address of President Buchanan. Mrs. Stevens died in 1952. On the death of her husband in 1955, the house and the square block of land on which it stands—half of the original lot—became the property of Mrs. Watson.

The white frame house is distinguished by the unusual and attractive arched treatment between the square columns of its railed veranda, which provides a graceful entrance to a central hall and airy rooms. The dwelling, which is in an excellent state of preservation, has been awarded a citation by the Historic American Buildings Survey as possessing exceptional historic or architectural interest.

William L. Callender house, one of Texas' best-preserved ante-bellum homes

Judge Alexander H. Phillips House

705 North Craig

LIKE MANY of its contemporaries, the Judge Alexander H. Phillips home, erected in 1851, was built of Victoria brick and cypress. It is a commodious two-story house with upper and lower porches extending across the entire front. There are two rows of six columns each supporting the porches, and the second-story veranda has a decorative railing. The house, which has been remodeled from time to time, is set in spacious grounds and surrounded by trees, shrubs, and flowers.

Judge Phillips, a prominent Victoria lawyer, was born in New York in the early 1800's and was educated at Union College, graduating in 1825. After having taught in the classical school of Lawrenceville, New Jersey, he moved to Texas. He began the practice of law in Galveston and Houston, but settled in Victoria in 1842. In 1866 he represented Victoria at, the state constitutional convention of that year, which produced a constitution soon ratified by the people but inoperative because of the state's being placed under military law by the federal government. Judge Phillips died in Victoria in 1880.

Following Judge Phillips' death, the home passed through a number of hands. His widow remarried and continued to live in the house with her second husband, Dr. Max Urwitz, until she moved to Houston. After that it became successively the property of J. K. Hexter; a Mr. Johnston, who opened the Johnston addition in Victoria; S. B. Dabney, a lawyer; W. N. Fleming, a ranchman; and Mrs. L. G. Kreisle. Finally it passed into the hands of its present owner, Dr. Walter W. Sale. Originally from Cuero, Dr. and Mrs. Sale have lived in the Phillips house for many years.

Not open to visitors.

Judge Alexander H. Phillips house, built in 1851 of Victoria brick

Tait Log House Ten miles south

Tait Town House Wallace Street

THE LOG CABIN on what was once Sylvania Plantation, now the Tait ranch, ten miles south of Columbus, bears unusually clear evidence of the year of its construction: the date 1847 is carved on two of its logs, one in the living room and one in the upstairs hall. The builder of the cabin, Dr. Charles William Tait, a graduate of William and Mary College, was both an engineer and a doctor. There is not much in the records to show that he practiced medicine after his arrival in Texas from Alabama, but for his engineering services to the government he was awarded six thousand acres of land, and upon this property he established his plantation.

The log cabin, which is still in use as ranch headquarters, is a notable example of Anglo-American frontier architecture. It is a story-and-a-half house of the improved dog-run type. Just under the roof at the front are long, narrow windows, formed by the omission of one log, that were planned as slits through which the occupants could shoot with safety. Though the house has two stairways, there was originally no entrance from the upstairs hall to the room where the children slept. For protection of the children, the only access to that room was from the one below where their parents slept. Only recently were the logs of the inner wall of the room sawed through to form a door from the hall.

The cabin has been moved three times. Several years ago, when it was transferred to higher ground, the entire structure was torn down log by log, and each log was treated for termites. The cabin was then rebuilt as it had been before. It has been photographed and dimensional drawings have been made for the permanent records of the Library of Congress.

FOR SOME YEARS after its construction the log house was the sole home of the Tait family. But yellow fever was bad in its location, and several children of the family died of the dread disease. The Taits then built a large house in the town of Columbus, and there four more children were born.

On May 12, 1956, the descendants of Dr. Charles William Tait welcomed guests at a celebration of the hundredth anniversary of the building of the town house. Construction was begun in 1856, although it was not completed until after the Civil War. The porches, which had not been finished before the war, were added when Dr. Tait returned from military service for the Confederacy, for which he had volunteered.

Simple columns of great dignity, two stories tall, support the roof of the mansion's front entrance porch, within which is a detached second-story balcony. In recent remodeling a back wing was added, with two porches supported by columns in the same style as those of the front porch but smaller in size. A new dining room with a marble floor opens onto one of these porches. A modern heating system has also been added, and there are now four baths and a powder room. In general plan, however, the main part of the house remains as it was in the early days.

Four tall chimneys, two at each end of the house, originally vented eight fireplaces. At one time the living room fireplace was rebuilt of stone from the Tait ranch, replacing the original red brick, but otherwise the fireplaces were restored just as they had been. In the most recent modernization of the house five of the eight fireplaces were left open for wood fires.

The Tait house is now owned and occupied by Mr. and Mrs. R. E. Tait and their family. Among their treasured possessions are early records of the plantation, showing that the land under cultivation at Sylvania, which in 1847 had been 1,907 acres, had increased by 1861 to more than 5,458 acres. The number of slaves grew in the same period from fifteen to sixty-three. Their value,

(Right) Charles William Tait log house, now used as the Tait ranch headquarters

(Below, right) Fireplace in living room

(Below, left) Hand-hewn log in living room showing date when house was built

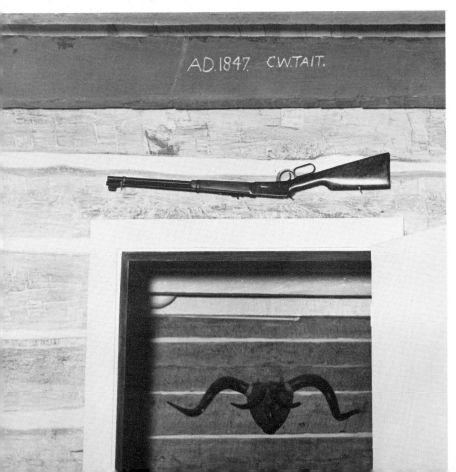

AD. 1847. C.W.TAIT.

which in 1850 was $10,000, had increased by 1863 to $31,000. It is said that Dr. Tait was a very kind master, who left the lash hanging unused in the stables. The plantation rules are still kept in the mansion, and a copy is also preserved in the library of the University of Texas at Austin. The "general rules," which reveal something of Dr. Tait's character as it was demonstrated in the management of his plantation, include these admonitions:

1st   Never punish a negro when in a passion. No one is capable of properly regulating the punishment for an offense when angry.

2nd   Never require of a negro what is unreasonable. But when you [have] given an order be sure to enforce it with firmness, yet mildly.

3rd   Always attempt to govern by reason in the first instance, and resort to force only when reason fails, and then use no more force than is absolutely necessary to procure obedience.

4th   In giving orders always do it in a mild tone, and try to leave the impression on the mind of the negro that what you say is the result of reflection.

5th   In giving orders be sure that you are understood, and let the negro know that he can always ask for an explanation if he does not understand you.

6th   When you are under the necessity of punishing a negro, be sure to let him know for what offense he is punished.

7th   Never act in such a way as to leave the impression on the mind of the negro that you take pleasure in his punishment. Your manner should indicate that his punishment is painful.

8th   A regular and systematic plan of operation is greatly promotive of easy government. Have all matters, therefore, as far as possible, reduced to a system.

9th   Negroes lack the motive of self-interest to make them careful and diligent, hence the necessity of great patience in the management of them. Do not therefore notice too many small omissions of duty.

10th   The maxim of making haste slow in plantation operations is equally applicable as in ordinary vocations of life. The meaning of which is not by attempting to do too much, to overwork and consequently injure your hands. Recollect that the journey of life is long and at best, a tedious one. The traveler, who wishes to make a long and safe trip, always travels in regular and moderate stages. Do not kill the goose to obtain the golden egg.

The Tait town house is open to visitors from 4 p.m. to 6 p.m. daily.

The Tait house in Columbus, one hundred years old in May, 1956

"Liendo"

Four miles east

LIENDO PLANTATION is associated most closely with the names of Elisabet Ney, the famous German sculptress, and Edmund Montgomery, her Scottish philosopher husband. But even before their arrival in Texas in 1873, the plantation had had a long and interesting history.

The property consisted of 1,100 acres, part of five leagues of land which the government of Mexico had assigned to José Justo Liendo in 1833 as a portion of eleven leagues he had purchased under the Colonization Law of 1828. For twenty years Liendo kept up the plantation; but in 1848 and 1849 he allowed the taxes on it to become delinquent. In 1850 Colonel Leonard W. Groce, son of the Texas patriot Jared Groce, bought the 7,240 acres involved in the tax litigation at public auction for $16.45. He also, however, paid Justo Liendo an additional $2,000 for the property.

In 1853 Leonard Groce built an elaborate plantation house on the Liendo land and moved his family there from the old Jared Groce home, "Bernardo." The new home, which Groce named "Liendo" for the former owner of the plantation, stood in a grove of live oaks near a bend of Pond Creek. For the construction of the Greek Revival house, a two-story white clapboard structure set on a red brick foundation, some $1,300 worth of lumber was cut from Georgia longleaf yellow pine and shipped to Houston, then taken by oxcart to the site. The Groce slaves made brick from the red Brazos clay for the wine cellar and some storage rooms. Three tall chimneys, one on each end of the house and one at the rear, vented six fireplaces, for three rooms downstairs and three just above. The roof was of heavy cedar shingles.

The balustered double veranda across the front of the house was supported by four tall square columns. Above this cool entrance, in the peak of the front gable, a bronze star was fixed with the date, 1853. The many windows lighted eleven large rooms, all with very high ceilings. Both floors had large central halls connected by a long flight of decorative stairs. An outside stairway gave easy access to the rear of the house.

All the interior walls were finished with smooth plaster. The floors and ceilings of random-width boards and dual-paneled doors were fashioned of yellow pine. The pilastered mantel in the immense living room was of black and gold marble; the other five mantels were black marble. Behind the large dining room, later partitioned to make a dining room and kitchen, were a sizable storeroom and a service pantry.

Flanking the main house were a number of slave cabins, tool sheds, smokehouses, barns, and other outhouses. There was a "bachelors' hall" for male guests, and a schoolhouse. The large kitchen was set apart from the main house about thirty feet. The whole establishment was planned to provide comfortable living for the large Groce family and to permit lavish hospitality.

When the Civil War came, the days of splendor ended. Before the war Colonel Groce's annual receipts from cotton had been from $80,000 to $100,000. But afterward the plantation which had been so profitable became an economic liability. In 1866 Colonel and Mrs. Groce sold "Liendo," with a thousand acres of land, to Mr. and Mrs. Philip S. Clarke, and moved to Galveston. The Clarkes were unable to operate the plantation profitably; and after a year they deeded the land back to the Groces and went away, leaving "Liendo" vacant. In 1868 Groce was declared bankrupt. In 1869 Mrs. Groce died, leaving her property to her son, Leonard W. Groce, Jr. And in 1873 the elder Groce also died.

Meanwhile, in 1871 Elisabet Ney, her husband, Edmund Montgomery, and "Cencie"—the daughter of an Innsbruck bookbinder who had become their housekeeper—came to America in search of a healthful climate for Montgomery, who suffered from tuberculosis. For two years they lived in Thomasville, Georgia; but the climate was not as good for Montgomery as they had hoped, and the

"Liendo," one of Texas' best-known ante-bellum plantation homes:
front gable has bronze star with date of building, 1853

couple's unconventional manners shocked their neighbors. At Elisabet's insistence Montgomery called her "Miss Ney," and she referred to him as her "best friend" rather than as her husband. There was much talk about their relationship, and when their first son, Arthur, was born the gossip became unbearable.

The Montgomerys had heard glowing reports of Texas, and decided to move there. Elisabet went ahead to find the sort of place they wanted. Robert Leisewitz, a Brenham cotton broker, told her of "Liendo," warning her at the same time of its unsoundness as an investment. But when Elisabet saw the plantation she was so enraptured by its beauty that she immediately gave Leonard Groce, Jr., her promise to buy and sent for Montgomery and Cencie. On March 4, 1873, Montgomery and Elisabet bought "Liendo" for $10,000, paying one-fourth in gold and promising to make two additional payments of $4,000 and $3,500 at stipulated intervals.

The furnishings they were able to provide for the spacious house were meager. They had a local carpenter make plain pine tables, stools, shelves, cots, and whatever else was absolutely essential. A study for Montgomery was arranged above the dining room, with crude furniture and a set of bookshelves to hold his books and papers. In this room, whose only piece of valuable equipment was a microscope, Montgomery resumed his research and philosophical writing.

Elisabet took over most of the work of running the plantation. She and Montgomery planned to keep quietly to themselves. But gossip had followed them from Georgia, and again their neighbors became suspicious—a suspicion greatly intensified when, during their first summer at "Liendo," Arthur died of diphtheria and his heartbroken parents, to avoid the danger of contagion, cremated the body in the living room fireplace without permitting anyone from outside to come near the house.

Against great odds, the Montgomerys tried to make a success of the plantation. But neither of them was practical enough to solve the complex economic problems involved. In spite of mounting debts they acquired more encumbered acres. During years of fumbling efforts they tried cotton, dairy and truck farming, and cattle ranching; but all proved unprofitable.

Finally, in 1891 Elisabet went to Austin to try to gain financial security for herself and her "best friend" through her work as a sculptress. Though she did not succeed in doing this, her work was well received. In the capitol building at Austin may be seen her sculptures of great Texans. In May, 1907, she suffered a severe heart attack. Montgomery went to Austin and nursed her devotedly for a month; but on June 29, she died. She was buried at "Liendo," in a grove of live oaks which she and Montgomery had planted.

Montgomery lived out his remaining years at "Liendo," disabled by a series of strokes and saddened by the failure of philosophers to recognize his work. Financial worries continued to plague him; and finally, in 1909, he sold "Liendo" to Theodore Low, reserving a 200-acre homestead for his use during his life. Low sold the property to W. P. Gaines, who in turn sold it to Captain and Mrs. G. W. Harris.

The Harrises moved in to occupy the house with Montgomery and Cencie. They proved to be kind and sympathetic friends, who did all they could to make Montgomery's last days comfortable. When he died, on April 17, 1911, they gave him "sepulture" beside his "faithful and devoted life-companion."

On the day of Montgomery's death Southern Methodist University was chartered. Twenty years later, on April 17, 1931, S.M.U. as custodian of the Montgomery Library, which Mrs. Harris had given the university in 1930, erected a bronze plaque at Montgomery's grave. And in 1936 the Texas Centennial Commission placed a marker near the old dwelling.

"Liendo" is now owned by Miss Willene Compton, who has done much to restore the historic plantation house to its former beauty.

Open to visitors by appointment.

Double veranda across
the front

The magnificent setting of
"Liendo"

Stagecoach Inn

North of business district

IN THE DAYS of the stagecoach, the stop at the settlement of Chappell Hill was the frame house which stands north of the business section where the old highway turned directly west. Chappell Hill, named for the pioneer Robert Chappell, was a trading post as early as 1849. In later years the spelling was changed to Chapel—allegedly by the officers of the Houston and Texas Central Railroad, who wanted to save paint and ink—but still more recently the town returned to the original spelling.

The Stagecoach Inn was built by William Hargrove and Jacob Haller in 1852. It was constructed of cedar and so arranged that some bedrooms and the dining room were on the first floor, together with the lobby and reception room. Upstairs more rooms for overnight guests were provided. The balusters of the stairs increase their height with each riser of the oak stairway. Interesting details are the cornice of Greek key design which encircles the house and the downspouts which bear the Lone Star of Texas, Imprinted in the copper downspout head is the date 1852, the year of the inn's construction.

William Hargrove brought his family to Texas in 1842 from Alabama. Several years later he formed a partnership with Jacob Haller for the purpose of operating an inn to provide accommodations for stagecoach passengers on the journey from Austin to Houston. After Haller's death Hargrove continued the operation of the inn with the assistance of his wife. Later, when death took her husband, Mrs. Hargrove sold the place to Judge Thomas; but it was run as an inn until the outbreak of the Civil War. Since then the house has been occupied by tenants. It has recently undergone extensive repairs.

In 1852, the same year that saw the building of the Stagecoach Inn, the Methodist church established Chappell Hill College as Chappell Hill Male and Female Institute. In 1856 the town took another step toward becoming an educational center with the establishment of Soule University for Boys, which was chartered that year to replace Rutersville and Wesleyan colleges. Chappell Hill College then became a school for girls, which existed until 1912. Soule University was closed during the Civil War and again later on because of a yellow fever epidemic, and was succeeded in 1875 by Southwestern University at Georgetown.

One pioneer settler has left a vivid description of the college activities at the close of the year. The Methodist Church was used by both Soule and Chappell Hill College as an auditorium, and a platform was built across its entire width. During the day oral examinations were held, and at night recitals were played on three pianos which had been placed on the improvised stage. On the final day a magnificent banquet was served. Huge cakes, some seven and eight layers tall, graced the tables; and one year peacock was served, a gift from Colonel W. W. Browning.

(Right) Cornice of Greek key design
encircling Stagecoach Inn

(Below) Stagecoach Inn, built in 1852 to
accommodate passengers on the journey
from Austin to Houston

Colonel W. W. Browning House

South of business district

THE BROWNING HOUSE in Chappell Hill is an example of the type of architecture which the early planters of Texas brought with them from their former homes in the southern states. It has the traditional gallery at front and back and the wide center hall running the length of the house with two large rooms on either side. Hand-hewn cedar woodwork, exceedingly heavy moldings over the doorway, and a well-preserved staircase are noteworthy details of this well-built plantation house.

Colonel W. W. Browning settled in Chappell Hill in the late 1850's. At first the family lived in a log house at the back of the plantation. When they started to build a new house, the first framework was blown down by a high wind; so at the second attempt the building was made doubly strong. While now in need of repair, the old home has stood while four generations occupied its spacious rooms.

Colonel Browning built up a large plantation and at one time owned over a hundred slaves. So sure was he that the southern cause would triumph in the Civil War that just before the close of the war he purchased more slaves. He was also a very devout man, who read his Bible every morning and night and assembled his family daily for prayers. At the age of five he promised his dying mother that he would never touch liquor, and that promise he kept even in illness.

Colonel Browning's daughter Sarah later took over the management of the plantation with her husband, Dr. Lockhart. A remarkable woman with a legal turn of mind, she is said to have read court decisions as a pastime. She was considered a natural executive and kept all the account books of the plantation for her husband, attending to the payment of all bills in the fall, the regular time for the settling of accounts on all plantations. When her husband went to war Sarah managed the large plantation, her judgment standing over that of the overseer—an unusual situation at a time when women were not generally considered capable in such matters.

In the years that have passed since the prosperous days of the plantations before the Civil War, time and change have taken their toll of the old Browning house. It is, however, still occupied.

Rear view of Browning house

(Below) Plantation home of
Colonel W. W. Browning

Seward Home

One mile east

THE RESIDENCE built by John Hoblett Seward and his wife, Laura Jane Seward, in 1855 stands a mile east of Independence—the town, originally Cole's Settlement, which was given its present name in 1836 to commemorate the signing of the Texas Declaration of Independence in neighboring Washington-on-the-Brazos. The home of Dr. Asa Hoxey, who proposed the naming of the town, was near by. Built in 1833, it is no longer standing, but a marker was placed at its site in 1936.

The Seward house was constructed almost entirely of cedar from trees growing within sight of the original location of the house, about a mile east of the spot where the old dwelling now stands. When it was found that the surroundings there were unhealthful, the house was rolled to its present location on cottonwood logs.

Slaves cut the timber for the house, then hauled it fifty miles to be milled. As ox teams were used to transport the material, the journey took a week each way. There was no architect, but among the slaves there were skilled carpenters, masons, and blacksmiths. The two-story part of the house is the original, the one-story portions having been added at various times. The structure rests securely upon a stone base. Its fireplaces were fashioned from native shale. The original shingle roof was re-placed in 1900. The lower and upper verandas shelter massive doorways with side lights and large shuttered windows. The house and yard, now beautifully restored, are surrounded by the traditional picket fence.

The double doors and wide reception hall lend the interior an air of gracious hospitality. Winding stairs are decorated with narrow white spindles; the treads, handrail, and newel are walnut. The floors are of cedar. Interior doors have decorative architraves. The house, in which only three modern bathrooms and the kitchen are of recent date, is furnished appropriately with priceless antiques.

Several generations have lived in the old home and have contributed to its preservation—John Hoblett Seward, Oscar A. Seward, Sr., and Clay I. Seward and his children. During 1955 the old Seward estate was divided, and the homestead became the property of Oscar A. Seward, Jr. He and his family now reside there.

This fine old home is one of those whose appearance and architectural features have been recorded for posterity by the Historic American Buildings Survey. In 1936 a Texas Centennial marker was placed in its front yard.

Open to visitors by appointment.

Two views of the John Hoblett Seward
house, lived in by the Seward family
since it was built in 1855

Anson Jones Home

Washington State Park

THE LAST WHITE HOUSE of the Republic of Texas was the simple story-and-a-half clapboard home built by President Anson Jones on his plantation near old Washington-on-the-Brazos. Named "Barrington" for the Massachusetts town where Jones was born in 1789, the house was built in 1844 during his candidacy for President by J. Campbell, who supervised the building of the house "& two log Cabins for 200 acres of Land $200 in cash and $100 in Stock at Market prices." Early in 1845 the President moved from the plantation of General James R. Cook, which he had rented from the General's widow, to his own three-hundred-acre plantation and new home.

Anson Jones's election to the Presidency climaxed a career which had begun unpromisingly with a series of failures as farmer and merchant in the East. After a brief stay in Venezuela and another in New Orleans, Dr. Jones arrived in Brazoria, Texas, in 1833, just at the end of an epidemic of Asiatic cholera. Two of the town's doctors had died in the epidemic, and others were needed. Dr. Jones remained, built up a good practice, and became a respected citizen of the town. In 1836 he participated in the Battle of San Jacinto while serving as a surgeon with the Texas forces. After the victory he became apothecary general of the army.

In 1837 Dr. Jones was elected representative from Brazoria to the Texas Congress. At the close of the session the next year he was sent by President Houston to Washington as Texas' minister plenipotentiary. Recalled in 1839 by President Lamar, to whose candidacy he had not been friendly, he found on his return to Texas that he had been elected to the Texas Senate to replace his old friend William Wharton, who had died. Then after a short period of return to the practice of medicine, he re-entered the service of the Republic in December, 1841, when President Houston, beginning his second term, appointed him secretary of state.

In 1844, during the agitation for annexation to the United States, Dr. Jones was elected President of the Republic. Though he had been opposed to annexation, he maneuvered skilfully to put Texas in the best position to bargain. Finally, on June 21, 1845, the Texas Congress voted for acceptance of the United States' annexation proposal. On July 4 a convention of delegates at Washington-on-the-Brazos adopted an ordinance accepting annexation. On February 19, 1846, President Jones lowered with his own hands the Lone Star Flag of Texas at the capitol at Austin. "The final act in this great drama is now performed," he said. "The Republic of Texas is no more."

From that time on Anson Jones retired to "Barrington," where he lived with his wife, who had been Mrs. Mary Smith McCrory, and their four children. He raised good corn and tobacco and premium cotton. But he was forced to endure constant pain in his left arm, which had withered after an injury in 1849, and he was lonely in retirement. In 1857 he suffered a crushing disappointment when he received not one vote in the Texas legislature to fill Sam Houston's Senate seat, a position for which he had been confident that he would be chosen. In despair he sold "Barrington" and set out for Galveston to take up once more the practice of medicine. But in Houston the thought of trying to begin again became more than he could endure, and he put a bullet through his head. Thus tragically ended a great and dramatic career.

In 1936 the Anson Jones house was purchased by the Centennial Commission and moved to the Washington State Park, where it is maintained by the Park Commission. Near by stands a replica of the building in which the Texas Declaration of Independence was written.

Open to visitors daily on same schedule as Washington State Park.

Home of Anson Jones, last President of the Republic of Texas

Fanthorp Inn

Main Street

ON THE OUTSKIRTS of Anderson, Fanthorp Inn, a substantial white frame house with double galleries, stands among moss-covered oak trees. Years ago this commodious inn welcomed and sheltered many travelers who rode the stagecoach from Houston to old Springfield, or from Nacogdoches to Austin. In the faded guest register are the names of such famous personages as Generals Lee, Jackson, Davis, and Grant.

In 1828 Henry Fanthorp, a wandering Englishman, came to Texas seeking new surroundings in which he might perhaps forget the death of his first wife in England and of his second wife in Virginia. The rolling lands of Southeast Texas appealed to him, and he lingered there, doing some trading and carpentry. Then he once more found companionship in the person of Rachel Kennard. They were married by bond—a marriage which, according to the Spanish law governing Texas at that time, had to be cemented by the first Catholic priest who came by. Meanwhile, the Rev. Daniel Parker, reputedly the first pastor of a Protestant church in Texas, performed the original ceremony.

Henry Fanthorp secured from the Mexican government several leagues of an original land grant known as "Alta Mira." Attracted by a grove of oak and cedar trees, Fanthorp built a commodious house about 1834 and presented it to his bride. Cedar trees from the grove provided the foundation—for which long, heavy beams from the felled trees were laid on their leveled stumps—and also much of the lumber for the entire building. Later the original rough logs were boarded over on both exterior and interior. The completed house contained thirty rooms. The east wing was used for the inn, the west side for family quarters, and the rear ell for the large kitchen and dining room.

About a hundred years ago the east wing of the house was torn down, leaving fourteen rooms for a family residence. From the spacious hall a stairway provides easy access to the gun closet below and the sleeping rooms above. The stair well and the gun closet are lined with half-hewn cedar logs of enormous sizes. The rooms have random-width puncheon floors, cut-log walls covered with wide boards, batten ceilings, and windows of varied sizes with many old panes. Other features of the old place are two cisterns, a well, and a novel arrangement of different floor levels.

In its days as a hostelry Fanthorp Inn not only accommodated many travelers, but also served as a post office and became a community center for news and politics. For a time it was used as a mercantile establishment. During the stormy days of revolution Sam Houston drilled troops in the front yard. In 1848 some officers of the United States army were billeted at the inn.

The town of Anderson was originally named Fanthorp. But when, in July, 1845, Kenneth L. Anderson, last Vice-President of the Republic, died at Fanthorp Inn on his way home from a session of Congress at Austin, the citizens of the town decided to honor his memory by changing the name of old Fanthorp to Anderson. The grave of Kenneth L. Anderson is not far from Fanthorp Inn.

The historic dwelling is now occupied by two direct descendants of Henry Fanthorp, Mrs. William Garber and her daughter, Mrs. Edward Buffington, and their families.

Not open to visitors.

Fanthorp Inn (before restoration), built in 1834 by
Henry Fanthorp, and occupied today by his descendants

Side view of Fanthorp Inn as it is today

Sam Houston's "Wigwam"

Campus of Sam Houston State Teachers College

SHELTERED BY AGED CATALPA TREES and surrounded by pecan trees and crepe myrtles, the simple white house that was Sam Houston's "Wigwam" stands today on the campus of Sam Houston State Teachers College as both a landmark and a historic shrine, visited each year by thousands of Texans. The college is the guardian of the local buildings that memorialize Houston. A wooded fifteen-acre tract contains not only the "Wigwam," but also the "Steamboat House," the law office, and the kitchen. On the same grounds stands the Sam Houston Memorial Museum, erected in 1936. Houston's grave is near by, in the Oakwood Cemetery.

The "Wigwam" is an excellent example of the transformation of a pioneer single log cabin into a comfortable six-room story-and-a-half house. Its back gallery with side rooms and several stone chimneys lend charm to the sturdy structure. To the original one-room cabin a second room was later added, with a "dog run" between. The porches were added still later, as were the attic and the drop siding. Wide board floors and square lead nails are indications of the age of the building in its earlier state.

The house, which was Sam Houston's favorite home, is largely furnished with household effects of the Houston family, supplemented by items appropriate to ante-bellum times. A rosewood piano dominates the parlor, where a large mirror reflects a sofa, a candle mold, a fluting iron at the mantel, and cyclone lamps. In the master bedroom a quilt of the Rose of Sharon pattern, which Mrs. Houston's mother, Mrs. Lea of Alabama, gave her daughter as a wedding gift, adorns a massive bed. A handloom, a trundle bed, and other pieces of furniture of Houston's time are also to be seen in the various rooms.

In the yard the restored log kitchen, set apart from the house according to custom, displays old cooking utensils around the hearth. Near by stands the small law office, also of logs, where Houston conferred with Texas dignitaries, with clients, and also with Indians such as Olooteka, the Cherokee chieftain.

Many tales have been told concerning Houston's penchant for whittling. It is said that he often carried a collection of carved hearts in his pockets. When he met an attractive lady he would gallantly offer her "his heart." Houston's habit of whittling necessitated the reflooring of the office in the yard of the "Wigwam," for the old floor had been chopped away piece by piece to save the owner from having to take many trips out of doors to replenish his stock of whittling sticks—or perhaps, sometimes, of fuel. In the house itself are to be seen such products of Houston's whittling art as a tiny ax whittled from a log, a small wooden bench, wooden buttons, and some odd charms that were carved in the Senate Chamber of the United States.

The use of the dog-run house as a shrine has been a matter of slow evolution. In 1890 Mrs. E. C. Smedes operated a popular boardinghouse for young ladies in the old "Wigwam." In 1910 the homestead was purchased by the students of Sam Houston Teachers College, who used the proceeds of an appearance by William Jennings Bryan at which he gave his famous oration, "The Prince of Peace," to erase the debt on the place. In 1927 the Texas legislature appropriated "$15,-000 for further restoration and maintenance of the old home." Today, under the enthusiastic supervision of Mrs. Grace Longino, Director of the Sam Houston Homes, Grounds and Museum, the entire fifteen acres and the memorial buildings are maintained and carefully tended. The grounds contain interesting collections of Texas plant life; and near the "Wigwam" still stands an old pecan tree that reputedly grew from a twig once plucked by Sam Houston for a saddle switch.

The house is open to the public daily from 9 a.m. to 5 p.m. There is no set admission fee, but a donation is welcome.

The "Wigwam" of
General Sam Houston

A corner of the "Wig-
wam's" living room

General and Mrs.
Houston's bedroom

Sam Houston's "Steamboat House"

Campus of Sam Houston State Teachers College

ON THE EVE of the Civil War, Sam Houston had sold his "Wigwam" and his "Raven Hill" plantation to locate in Independence. When he refused to take the oath of allegiance to the Confederacy and was therefore deposed as governor of Texas, he returned to Huntsville and bought the "Steamboat House."

Dr. Rufus Bailey had built the house in 1858, designing it to look like a Mississippi steamer with lower and upper decks. Dr. Bailey intended to give the unusual structure to his son Frank and his bride as a wedding present, but the two young people disliked it so much that they refused to live in it.

Nevertheless, the house was built well and possessed a number of attractive features. It is supported by long beams that are twelve inches square. The exposed rafters and thick sleepers are also a foot wide. Square-headed nails fasten the wide drop siding. The steep entrance stairs, rising between the two towers or turrets which were used as gun cabinets and closets, reach from the ground to the second floor, sheltering a porch-opening for the first floor.

Behind the twin towers upper and lower decks, long and wide, extend the entire length of the house on both sides. The rooms which open on these decks have doors rather than windows, so that there is a private outside entrance for each room. In the outside doors original hand-scratched glass in small panes provides both lighting and decoration.

The rooms with their random flooring, boarded walls, and batten ceilings are furnished appropriately with pieces that were originally Houston's or that came from other homes of his time. The most arresting feature in the entire house is the handsome portrait of Houston that commands the parlor. Over the parlor fireplace, flanked by a pair of old sofas, hangs a good portrait of Mrs. Houston. A double-faced desk, several huge beds, and warming pans are among the other interesting nineteenth-century furnishings.

In this house Houston spent his last years, concerned about the future of his adopted state and the fate of his son, who had joined the soldiers in gray to fight for a cause which he considered futile. In 1863 the old warrior died in a lower bedroom of the "Steamboat House." His body lay in state in the upper parlor, and then was carried down the steep steps to its burial in Oakwood Cemetery.

A succession of owners followed for the "Steamboat House." In 1879 Major T. J. Goree, who owned the house at that time, gave a large dinner for the opening of the Sam Houston Normal Institute. Among other notables the party included Governor O. M. Roberts, Dr. O. H. Cooper, and Congressman Roger Q. Mills. At the dinner plans were discussed for the opening of the long-awaited University of Texas, which was finally established four years later.

In 1936 J. E. Josey presented the "Steamboat House" to the state of Texas, and it was moved to its present location on the campus of Sam Houston State Teachers College.

Open daily to visitors from 9 a.m. to 5 p.m. No admission fee is charged, but a donation is welcome.

(*Above*) Parlor of the "Steamboat House" with portraits
of General and Mrs. Houston

(*Below*) "Steamboat House," built to resemble a Mississippi steamer

Noble House

Sam Houston Park

THE LAST HOUSE remaining from the days of the Republic of Texas in Houston, once capital of that Republic, is the A. W. Noble house, built in 1842 on a point overlooking Buffalo Bayou in what is now Sam Houston Park. The builder of the house was Nathaniel K. Kellum, who in 1841 bought the twenty-acre farm on which he planned to erect the dwelling. Bricks for the construction of the house were brought by Kellum's slaves from his own brickyard on the bayou.

The house was the first two-story brick home in Houston. A most unusual detail was that Kellum built the house without an inside stairway. He simply set a ladder against a second-story window.

Kellum did not complete the house, but sold it in 1850 to Mr. and Mrs. A. W. Noble of Liberty County. When it was finished, the house was encircled by broad, shady porches, the upper one railed, with brick columns below and slender, graceful wooden ones above. An outside stairway at the rear gave access to the upper gallery. The Louisiana-French influence was to be felt in the architecture of the home, which was admirably suited to the Houston climate.

The house was not only a home, but also one of the city's first private schools. In February, 1851, an advertisement appeared in the *Democratic Telegraph and Texas Register,* announcing that

Mrs. Noble and Miss Kelly will open a school on Monday, February 10th, at the large, airy and commodious house . . . universally known as the late residence of N. K. Kellum, for the instruction of Misses generally, and Masters under the age of twelve, in the various branches of an English education with Drawing, Painting, Worsted Embroidery, and Music if required. Pupils wishing to board with the Teachers, can be accommodated.

At the end of the Civil War, the house became the headquarters of the Sam Houston Military Academy. In 1899 it was bought by Mayor Sam Brashear for the city of Houston, and the city's first park, Sam Houston Park, was established on its grounds. The house became a historical museum, and later a zoo was built in its back yard— an enterprise which was shortly abandoned because of the $200-a-month food bill it entailed. Houston's first open air concerts were given from a bandstand on the lawn. The house was also used as the residence of the park caretaker.

The Noble house has always been surrounded by majestic trees. The age of some has been estimated at three hundred years. Unhappily, hurricanes have destroyed some of the oldest.

For several decades the house suffered from neglect, and on several occasions it was actually condemned by the city. But the appeals of interested citizens such as Mrs. E. Richardson Cherry, a connoisseur of artistic and historic values, saved the old landmark. The movement for the preservation and restoration of the house has culminated in the work of the Harris County Heritage and Conservation Society, which has undertaken the task of restoring it carefully and accurately to its early state. The interior is being furnished with authentic period pieces. On March 2, 1956, a flag-raising ceremony marked the opening of the restored Noble house.

Open to visitors daily.

A. W. Noble house

Cherry House

608 Fargo

IN AUGUST, 1956, the Houston City Council approved plans for the transfer of the Cherry house, already one of the most frequently moved of early Texas homes, to a permanent location in Sam Houston Park near the Noble house. The park was designated as a future depository for historically important homes of Houston—an "outdoor museum" of houses.

The Cherry house was built in 1850 by General E. B. Nichols on Quality Hill across from the old courthouse. General Nichols' partner was Colonel Pierce, who was manager of a fleet of ships that sailed between New York and Texas. When Nichols decided to make his home in Houston, he used for his house lumber which was reputedly designated first for a ship. Hence, it was unusually strong and durable. The sills which ran the length of the structure were eighteen to twenty-four inches square, and were mortised and fastened with wooden pegs and handmade nails. The puncheon floors throughout the house were three inches thick. Studdings were treated with a preservative of heavy tar.

The details of the fine Georgian home were carefully executed for beauty and endurance. Eight massive Ionic columns supported two front galleries, lower and upper. Some thirty-eight decorative hand-carved windows and numerous doors with wrought-iron hinges added charm to both the exterior and the interior of the mansion. A handsome staircase with hand-carved rose brackets led from the high-ceilinged lower rooms to the spacious second floor. August Bering, a well-known Houston builder, has told of the work he did as a fifteen-year-old apprentice to the master carver who created the graceful ornamentation of the house, sharpening the master's chisels and himself doing bits of carving.

Before the house was finished, Nichols moved to Galveston. He sold the structure to William Marsh Rice, whose name is perpetuated in Rice Institute; Rice moved it to the corner of San Jacinto and Franklin and there completed it, carrying out the original plans that had been made for such details as wainscoting and balustrades. The home cost some $8,000, which was a goodly sum in those days.

The next owner of the house was Captain Charles Evershade, who was one of the original Morgan Line captains. Then in 1886, when the old City Bank of Houston had failed and real estate values had gone down, John D. Finnegan, a dealer in hides and leather, bought the old dwelling. Eight years later he asked for sealed bids on the house. Mrs. E. Richardson Cherry became interested in the structure, and her husband submitted a bid of $25.00 for the classic front door. The bid, which was the only one submitted, was accepted for the entire house on condition that it be speedily moved away.

The Cherrys owned a small tract of land south of town, and to it they moved their handsome acquisition. The transfer cost $450 and consumed forty-six nights in 1894. When the house finally arrived at its new location, it was found that not even a brick in the chimney had shifted from its place. For many years the Cherry family enjoyed the use of the house as a home and private art studio. Mrs. Cherry, a spirited artist, helped to establish the Houston Public Art League, the forerunner of the Houston Art Museum, and retained her vigorous interest in the artistic life of the city until her death at the age of ninety-five.

In 1932, when the Historic American Buildings Survey studied and photographed the historic homes of Texas, it included the Cherry house in its listing of authentic colonial homes remaining in the Houston area. Mrs. Dorothy Cherry Reid recently gave the home of her late parents to the Harris County Heritage and Conservation Society, which is making plans for its restoration and preservation in Sam Houston Park.

Open to visitors daily.

(Right) Beautifully carved doorway of the Cherry house; *(below)* E. Richardson Cherry house originally built on "Quality Hill"

Charles H. Milby House

614 Broadway

DURING THE CIVIL WAR the Milby family erected a dignified and imposing mansion in the pioneer town of Harrisburg, then a busy village, now part of Houston. When it was completed in 1864, the home of Charles H. Milby was a typical plantation structure, elongated and two-story. From the upper gallery one could see stern-wheel and side-wheel boats as they plied on the Bayou between Houston and the coast, carrying passengers and cargo. Not far away a narrow wooden bridge spanned Bray's Bayou on the busy road to Houston.

Mrs. Milby's father, John Grant Todd, was an active stockholder in Texas' first railroad company, the Buffalo Bayou, Brazos, and Colorado Railroad. At first it seemed that this new enterprise would make a bustling city of little Harrisburg. But in 1870 the pioneer line became a part of the Galveston, Harrisburg, and San Antonio Railroad, and the consolidated line's shops were moved to Houston. Harrisburg's population was sharply reduced almost over night. Many of the railroad workers tore down their houses, carried the building materials and their household effects to Houston, and rebuilt their homes in the environs of the Southern Pacific shops.

Houston's Broadway was even then a wide and busy thoroughfare. People walked in the footpath in its center; and when the street was finally paved an esplanade for pedestrians was constructed.

Before this walkway was removed, merchants along Broadway often protested that the parking of vehicles along the curb made it impossible for pedestrians to see the wares exhibited in their shop windows.

During the busy 1880's Charles H. Milby improved his home to keep abreast of the times. In 1885 he remodeled and enlarged the old house. The brick walls, now covered with concrete blocks, were adorned on two sides with galleries bearing highly ornamented posts and railings. A glassed conservatory occupied one corner. More than a hundred shutters protected French windows. The Milby mansion in its new state was one of the finest homes on Broadway, and many lavish parties were given there.

Today the upper galleries afford commanding views of Houston, the ship channel, and surrounding business structures. The Milby home stands in the center of a great industrial area which far surpasses the wildest dreams that the builders of Harrisburg cherished for their village a century ago. The old dusty—or muddy—road with its bothersome pedestrian lane has been transformed into a wide thoroughfare over which flows a stream of motor traffic. The Milby landmark, entrenched behind its brick and iron fence and its ancient trees and shrubbery, bridges the gap between the days of the Civil War and the modern age.

Charles H. Milby house: upper galleries overlook surrounding business structures

Hogg Home: "Varner Plantation"

Two miles northwest

NEAR WEST COLUMBIA, in a beautiful setting of moss-draped trees, stands a plantation house the original part of which is more than a century and a quarter old. Exactly when the main house and cellar were built is legend, but parts of the structure probably date back to 1824 or 1825. The "Varner Plantation" is located on the old Martin Varner League, one of the first grants in Stephen F. Austin's first colony.

Among the early settlers of Columbia was a wealthy Mississippian, William H. Patton, who established and for many years maintained a prosperous sugar plantation on Varner Creek. Beginning where the Varners had left off, Patton built an imposing colonial mansion of brick, stucco, and wood. The architraves of the doors and windows were similar to those of the Governor's Mansion in Austin, and the story goes that the same wandering Irish carpenter fashioned the decorative facings for both houses.

The plantation was well equipped, with a large sugar house containing double sets of kettles; slave cabins built of brick made on the place; an umbrella-shed lined with benches, where the slaves came to eat; and a stable and race track for the shelter and exercising of the thoroughbred horses raised on the estate. Lovely yards and cultivated fields surrounded the plantation house.

In 1901 the plantation was purchased by James Stephen Hogg, who has been called "the most conspicuous and spectacular character in State affairs since the days of Sam Houston." Hogg, the first native Texan to serve as governor of the state, held that office from 1891 to 1895. A strong reform governor, one of whose great achievements was the creation of the Railroad Commission of Texas, Hogg carried out his controversial policies with such vigor and determination that the campaign for his second term, in 1892 against George W. Clark, was one of the most hotly fought in Texas history.

Before Hogg's death from an injury received in a railroad accident in 1906, he advised his family to hold fast to "the Varner," prophesying that oil would be found under the old sugar fields. The prophecy was fulfilled in 1917, and today tall derricks are scattered throughout the old plantation grounds.

In 1920 the house was restored and some alterations were made. On the creek side of the house the two galleries, on the first and second floors, were retained; but on the front elevation six stately ground-to-roof columns replaced the earlier arrangement. A new kitchen was made from the original servants' porch and hall, and a partition was removed between the old kitchen and dining room, to create a new dining room of commodious proportions.

Lost in the remodeling was the old wash shed where the slaves once gathered to wait for their meals. The wooden tower which had supported the plantation bell was also removed; but the bell itself is still in use. Recurring storms have damaged many of the dependencies of the plantation. The sugar mill was demolished in 1900, and practically all the slave quarters were lost some ten years later.

Governor Hogg's children, Will, Mike, Tom, and Miss Ima, have continued their father's care of the plantation. Will brought in the first oil well. Miss Ima and Will have devoted much time to the furnishing and maintenance of the house. Family heirlooms adorn many rooms. Miss Ima, whose deep interest in the preservation of Texas landmarks is attested by her work as a member of the Texas State Historical Survey Committee, has for many years maintained the old home for her own use and for public visits during the Pilgrimage at West Columbia.

Open to visitors during Pilgrimage at West Columbia in April.

"Varner Plantation," home of James Stephen Hogg: *(below)* front view of house; *(right)* detail of doorway

Thomas Jefferson Chambers House

Cummings Street

AT THE HEAD of Trinity Bay in Anahuac, once called Chambersea, stands the restored home of General Thomas Jefferson Chambers, built in 1845. The wide-eaved two-story house, with its unique circular staircase rising from the lower veranda to the upper, is quaint and sturdy. The two verandas shelter identical entrances with double doors which, like the large windows, are equipped with shutters.

In 1834 Chambers, who had served since 1829 as surveyor-general of Texas, was appointed judge of the Superior Court at a salary of $3,000 a year. When the Republic came into existence, however, its treasury contained no funds for the salaries of officials; and Chambers, along with others, was forced to accept land in lieu of money as payment for his services. Although the Republic received large sums of money from the sale of lots from this same land, it was not until 1925 that Chambers' heirs were compensated for their claim to the capitol grounds in Austin and a large portion of the property on which the city itself is located.

Early in 1835, Anahuac became the scene of one of the preliminary battles of the Texas Revolution. Santa Anna sent a company of soldiers to Fort Anahuac, which was used as both fort and customs house, to assist in the collection of duties.

Thereupon William B. Travis and a force of colonists marched on the fort, captured it, and made the Mexicans surrender their arms and leave for San Antonio.

During the Revolution Chambers recruited soldiers for Texas in the North. At the entrance to the capitol building in Austin today stand two cannons which bear the inscription: "Presented to the Republic of Texas by Major T. J. Chambers."

After having led a dramatic life, Chambers met a sudden and tragic death in 1865 when an unknown assassin shot him through a window of his home as he sat inside with his family. Tradition has since added that the bullet which pierced Chambers' body crossed the room and penetrated his portrait at exactly the same spot.

For a time the Chambers house fell into disrepair. But the public-spirited citizens of Anahuac, recognizing the historical significance of the structure, restored it to its original and architecturally interesting form. They then established the Chambers County Library within its walls. The Chambers County Memorial Fund materially aided the project.

Open daily Monday through Friday, 9 a.m. to 5 p.m., and Saturday 10 a.m. to 12 noon.

Thomas Jefferson Chambers house, built in 1845

Menard House: "The Oaks"

1603 Thirty-third

WHEN MICHEL BRANAMOUR MENARD, founder of Galveston, formed the Galveston City Company in 1836 and laid out the town, he reserved ten acres in the southwest part of the city for his own home. There, in 1840, he built "The Oaks," named for the grove of oak trees he himself had nurtured on what had previously been bare land. All of Galveston Island, for that matter, had been barren and unoccupied since Jean Lafitte and his band of pirates had left it in 1821. The sandy island had been used for landings by officials of the Mexican government, which did not permit colonists to settle on the Texas coast. The Texas Republic, on the other hand, encouraged settlement there; and Menard obtained from the first Texas Congress a league (about 4,439 acres in the Spanish measurement) and a labor (about 177 acres) at a cost of $50,000.

For his house, Menard had pine timbers and Ionic columns shipped from Maine, and sills of pine brought from Florida and Georgia. The house was mortised throughout, and the joists were set in white lead. The Greek Revival style was followed in the architectural design. The two-story house was originally square, but later side wings and a rear ell were added, in the same style as the central portion.

Today, the lower floor contains an entrance hall. A bedroom in one wing and a dining room in the other are shaded by columned porches, as is the front entrance. The rear ell with its long porch provides additional space. On the second floor, just off the center hall, a partially shuttered airway, unique in plan, furnishes a comfortable outdoor room for family living. There are also four upstairs bedrooms. Only modern plumbing and a few closets have been added of late years to the spacious old home.

Born in 1805 in Canada of French parents, Michel Menard became associated with the American Fur Company and ultimately managed an extensive fur business. He made friends with many of the Indians whom he met in the course of his work, and learned their customs and their language. His expert horsemanship and his skill with the bow and arrow, as well as with the rifle, so impressed the Indians that they looked upon him as a superman; and eventually he became a chieftain of the Shawnees. Then, in 1829, he went to Texas.

Menard's knowledge of and experience with the Indians were invaluable to Texas, for when the Revolution against Mexico broke out he used his influence to prevent the Texas tribes from joining the Mexican cause. He was also a signer of the Texas Declaration of Independence, and served in the Congress of the Republic. The exchequer system which he devised saved the Republic from bankruptcy.

Menard lived in "The Oaks" until his death at the age of fifty-one, when the home became the property of his wife and their young son, Doswell. In 1885 the property was sold to Edward N. Ketchum, who restored it. During the Galveston flood, the Ketchum family recalls, neighbors flocked to the second floor of the stout structure. When the water receded, the storm-weary refugees discovered a cow in the parlor, which was littered with soaked sheets of wallpaper. The front yard was covered with uprooted oaks and flood debris. No vital damage was done, however, and the house was soon restored to its full beauty. It has remained in the Ketchum family during the succeeding half-century. H. R. Ketchum is the present owner of this proud old landmark of Galveston.

Not open to visitors.

(Left) Column detail of "The Oaks"

(Below) Home of Michel Branamour Menard, founder of Galveston

(Below, left) Setting of "The Oaks," named after trees
nurtured by Michel Menard

Williams-Tucker House

3601 Avenue P

AT PRESENT a one-story frame house, the home which Samuel May Williams, one of Galveston's founding fathers, built in 1839-40 originally possessed also a ground floor containing a large brick kitchen with a brick fireplace and oven, and a brick wine cellar and provision room. The bricks for this part of the house were brought from Baltimore as ballast in vessels which were loaded with cotton on their return trip. The ground-floor rooms, however, along with the seven-foot brick piers which support the house, disappeared almost completely (some parts are still visible) in 1905-6 when a grade-raising fill was ordered to help prevent a repetition of the damage caused by the disastrous Galveston flood of 1900.

The house, which now faces its neighbor instead of the street, was built on a ten-acre lot which at that time was outside the Galveston city limits. The main part was framed in Saccarrappa, Maine, of northern white pine and hemlock, and shipped to Galveston ready to be set up. The trim was of Texas longleaf pine. Originally the house was crowned by a gallery and central cupola, but after these features were destroyed by fire in the 1890's they were replaced by flat decking.

Samuel May Williams, a native of Baltimore, spent several years of his youth in Mexico, where he learned to speak Spanish. In Mexico he met Jared Groce, who persuaded him to go to Texas. Arriving in 1822, he was appointed secretary to Austin's colony, "because he was fluent in the use of French and Spanish, wrote a fine Spencer-ian hand, and was a tireless worker." He kept all land records, served as Austin's assistant, and later aided him as co-empresario.

Williams soon went on to another partnership, this time with Thomas F. McKinney. As a result of this association he became a successful merchant in Quintana, an early-day settlement at the mouth of the Brazos River. In 1827 the firm was moved to Galveston. A few years later it obtained a charter as a bank and was authorized to issue $30,000 in paper to circulate as currency. Williams could thus lay claim to the title of first banker in Texas.

With McKinney and Michel Menard, Williams formed the Galveston City Company. It was the good fortune of Texas' leading port to be promoted by a company which pressed the development of its harbor facilities "in the face of several discouraging storms and the depreciation of shares in the company to ten cents on the dollar." It is said that Williams made the arrangements for the first export shipment of goods to leave Galveston for a European port.

The Williams home was purchased in 1859 by Phillip C. Tucker, and for more than ninety years it was occupied by the Tucker family. Now the Galveston Historical Foundation has chosen the house as its first project in preservation and restoration. Having purchased the old dwelling, the Foundation started work on the project on April 21, 1956.

Open to visitors daily.

Williams-Tucker house, framed in Maine and shipped to Galveston to be set up

Henry Rosenberg House

1306 Market

AN EXAMPLE of a century's transition from early Galveston architecture through the Victorian mode to the Modern Colonial style may be seen in the two-story Rosenberg house. Built in 1859 in a spirit of dignified simplicity, it originally had four large chimneys and a glass-enclosed "captain's cupola" such as many dwellings possessed in the seaport towns of that day. Later, typically Victorian jigsaw scrolls were added on the front gallery and above some of the windows. Today, shorn of this ornamentation and without the cupola, the limestone house shows its structural soundness through clean lines that give it a modern appearance.

The original interior was richly handsome. Tall white Corinthian columns separated the double parlors. Ceilings displayed medallions carved in grape and leaf design. Eight Italian marble fireplaces featured keystones of fruit and flowers. Rosewood cornices stippled in gold leaf enhanced the floor-length windows, the lower panels of which opened like doors. Ornamental grillwork over the doors was designed to hold potted plants.

Originally the Rosenberg property extended almost to Fourteenth Street. On that side was a two-story brick carriage house, which later became a clubhouse for the United Daughters of the Confederacy. To the east, behind the main house, was the servants' house, also a two-story brick building.

Henry Rosenberg, born in Switzerland, arrived in Galveston as a youth of some sixteen or seventeen years. During his lifetime he amassed a fortune as a merchant and banker. He is remembered for his many and varied gifts to Galveston. Rosenberg built a public school at a cost of some $60,000 and presented it to the city. In his will he made bequests to the Island City Protestant and Israelitish Orphan Home, for building purposes; to the Episcopal Grace Church parish, for a church building; to the Ladies' Aid Society of the German Lutheran Church, for their use for charitable purposes; to the Woman's Home of Galveston, for an appropriate building; and to the Young Men's Christian Association of Galveston, for the purchase or erection of a building. He also provided money for the erection of "not less than ten drinking fountains for man and beast," and of a monument to the memory of the heroes of the Texas Revolution. This monument, the work of the sculptor Louis Amateis, now stands at the corner of Broadway and Rosenberg Avenue. It was unveiled on San Jacinto Day in 1900.

But perhaps the bequest touching most closely the lives of the people of Galveston was that for the organization and endowment of a free public library. The Italian Renaissance building, which was built some four years after the erection of the monument, houses 100,000 volumes. It also contains an important Texana collection which includes over fifty personal letters of Stephen F. Austin, as well as papers and documents signed by Houston, Jackson, Lincoln, Grant, and Jefferson Davis. The library represents the realization of the donor's desire, expressed in a statement appended to his will:

I desire to express in practical form my affection for the city of my adoption and for the people among whom I have lived for so many years, trusting that it will aid their intellectual and moral development, and be a source of pleasure and profit to them and their children, and their children's children, through many generations.

Long a palatial residence, the Rosenberg house has now been converted into comfortable apartments.

Not open to visitors.

Henry Rosenberg house: two changes in a century of transition

George Ball House

1405 Twenty-fourth

AN UNUSUAL and highly decorative Doric frieze is a striking feature of the George Ball house, built in 1857, which with its four two-story columns of the same order provides an impressive example of the Greek Revival style in early Texas architecture. The carved architraves of the tall windows and ornate doors add to the charm of a house which even now, when it is crowded by buildings on either side, retains its classic dignity. Behind the columns is the ornate rail of a private second-story balcony.

The house was strongly built of Maine pine. The floors of the interior, like those of the verandas, were constructed of broad boards put together with pegs. Balusters of the handsome stairs were octagonally fluted, matching the central portion of the newel. In its original plan, the mansion contained spacious rooms for entertaining downstairs and airy bedrooms above.

A native of New York State, George Ball set out at the age of twenty-one literally to seek his fortune. After traveling throughout the western and southern states, he settled for a time in Shreveport, Louisiana. Then he began to hear interesting rumors of Texas, and finally he decided that he would cast his lot with the young Republic. Going back to New York, he formed a partnership with his brother. Together the two brothers bought enough building materials to erect a store, and a stock of merchandise to sell in it. Thus equipped, Ball set sail for Galveston.

He could scarcely have arrived in that town of 1,500 inhabitants at a more inopportune time. An epidemic of yellow fever was raging, and people were not in a mood to take much interest in a new business establishment. Nevertheless, Ball leased a lot on Tremont and set about starting his store. A year later his brother joined him, and so successful were the partners that soon the business was moved to a more desirable location at Strand and Twenty-second.

Presently George Ball and John Sealy became associated in banking, shipping, and wholesale operations. In 1854 Ball reorganized his affairs to enter the firm of Ball, Hutchings and Company, a mercantile business which included the brothers John and Robert Sealy. The firm became a leading Galveston institution and important in financial matters throughout the state. During the Civil War it carried on a lively business with Mexico. And through the succeeding years of Reconstruction and panic it continued to meet all its obligations.

Ball, a Galveston civic leader, was particularly interested in the development of the island city's transportation facilities. He is said to have been the first to subscribe $10,000 worth of stock in the Mallory Steamship Company. Like Henry Rosenberg, he also wished to make a useful contribution to the city during his lifetime. He bought land and erected a school, which was given his name—the George Ball High School. For the land, the building, and the equipment, Ball and his heirs reputedly spent more than $100,000. Ball also left in the hands of his executors the sum of $50,000, the interest on which was to be used for the poor and needy of the city.

Originally the Ball home was located on the northwest corner of Tremont Street and Avenue I, where the Rosenberg Public Library now stands. In the late 1860's George Ball sold the house to P. J. Willis, Sr., who engaged with his brother in a large wholesale business. After the death of P. J. Willis, his daughter, Mrs. J. G. Goldthwaite, lived in the house for many years. In 1901 the Ball residence was sold at public auction for $500 to John Focke to make room for the Rosenberg Library building. The old structure was then moved onto two lots owned by Focke on Twenty-fourth Street between M and M½, and was divided into two dwellings. The house is now owned by Mrs. P. E. McKenna. It is one of the historic homes of early Texas which are registered in the Library of Congress.

(Right) Stairway in Ball house: octagonally fluted balusters and newel

(Below) George Ball house, built in 1857

John Sealy House

822 Tremont

IN THE EARLY 1860's John Sealy, who was George Ball's associate in a prosperous mercantile and banking business, built a house facing Ball's on the corner of Tremont Street and Avenue I. At first a modest frame house, it was soon converted into an impressive residence of cut stone and polished wood, with front and side verandas and second-floor galleries, and with long rows of tall white Ionic columns. French doors, wide windows, and ornate gables added charm to the commodious home, as did the carved cornices beneath the lofty eaves. The large rooms of the interior were elaborately furnished. In this home John Sealy, his wife Rebecca, and their two children, John Sealy and Jennie Sealy Smith, spent the greater part of their lives.

John Sealy, who was born in Pennsylvania in 1822, traveled to Galveston at the age of twenty-four and became a clerk in the Henry Hubbell & Company dry goods store. J. H. Hutchings was a bookkeeper at that store, and in 1847 Sealy and Hutchings formed a business firm called Hutchings & Company and moved to Sabine Pass. In 1854 Hubbell decided to go out of business. Sealy and Hutchings then bought his store, and with George Ball formed the firm of Ball, Hutchings & Company. Soon they turned from the mercantile aspect of the business to banking, and their firm exists today as the oldest bank in Texas, the Hutchings Sealy National Bank.

John Sealy was the first member of his family to leave a part of his fortune for purposes of medical education. The city of Galveston offered a block of land and the executors of Sealy's estate offered an endowment of $50,000 if the state would locate the medical branch of the University of Texas in Galveston. The John Sealy Hospital was built in 1890 at a cost of nearly $90,000, exclusive of furnishings and equipment, and the Medical Branch opened in 1891.

Since that time the family has given millions of dollars for the teaching hospitals which have served the University. Rebecca Sealy left a bequest of $10,000,000, "the principal of which was to be used for the construction of buildings and equipment for the advancement of science and the betterment of mankind." A nurses' residence was constructed in Mrs. Sealy's memory. John Sealy, Jr., continued the family contributions to the cause of medicine, expending some $250,000 for improvements on the hospital. With his sister, Jennie Sealy Smith, he added a women's building to the hospital at a cost of $135,000. In 1922 the brother and sister established the Sealy and Smith Foundation, which, with a substantial endowment, will provide funds for the hospitals in perpetuity.

Another Sealy home, that of George Sealy, John Sealy's brother and business associate, stands at 2424 Broadway. Often called "The Open Gates," this mansion was built in 1889 in French Renaissance style. It has welcomed such celebrities as Clara Barton and President Benjamin Harrison.

The John Sealy house is now the property of the First Baptist Church, which uses the building for offices and Sunday school rooms.

(Below) Home of John Sealy, one of Galveston's greatest benefactors; *(right)* detail of the tall Ionic columns and carved cornice

Powhattan House

3427 Avenue O

THE POWHATTAN HOUSE was Galveston's first family hotel. It failed financially, however, because in its original location on Twenty-first Street between Avenues M and N it was too far from town. The hotel was built in 1847 for John S. Sydnor, who was one of Galveston's early mayors. Choosing the impressive and popular Greek Revival style, Sydnor constructed the building with lumber, brick, and Doric columns all brought from Maine. The columns, five feet in circumference and almost forty feet tall, were shipped in sections on a sailing vessel. The hotel had twenty-four rooms with ceilings fifteen feet high and windows four feet wide. Each of the rooms had a brick or stone fireplace. The structure rested on a foundation which raised it ten feet above the ground.

Colonel Sydnor, who moved to Galveston from Virginia in 1838, possessed an unusual degree of versatility and initiative. For another house he built in Galveston, the structure on Avenue I which later became known as "Heidenheimer's Castle," he experimented with reef shell and cement to make what proved to be a thoroughly satisfactory and lasting concrete. This is said to be the first such concrete house. Sydnor was also the first to cultivate oysters in Galveston waters. During his administration as mayor, in 1846-47, Galveston's first city market was built and the Police and Fire Department was organized. He was instrumental in starting a free public school system for Galveston—which, however, collapsed after a few successful years because the aldermen failed to levy taxes for its support.

For a time the Powhattan House was the home of Colonel Sydnor, whose daughter, Columbia, was married there. Then it was sold to a Mr. Bol-

ton, who used the building for a school. At first both boys and girls were admitted, but later the school became a military academy. When this venture, too, proved unsuccessful, Mr. Bolton turned the building once more into a residence, which he occupied.

In 1881 the structure passed into the possession of the city of Galveston for use as an orphanage. It served in that capacity until 1893, when Henry Rosenberg willed the city a sum of money for a new orphanage. Mrs. Caroline Willis Ladd then purchased the old hotel and moved it to a block of land between Thirty-fourth and Thirty-fifth. She divided the building into three houses. The main section stands today at Thirty-fifth and Avenue O. In 1903 Charles Vedder bought this part of the original hotel, as his home, and it remained in his family until 1935, when J. W. Oshman became the owner.

Even though the house is now an abbreviated version of the original plan of the builder, it still contains the original doorway, stairway, and parlors. When it was moved and remodeled, it was placed on a high brick basement. The three tall Doric columns and the iron-railed overhanging balcony give dignity to the exterior. The first floor plan provides for a stair hall, two living rooms, a dining room, a kitchen, and a storage room. The southwest living room is notable for its beamed ceiling. The second story contains five rooms.

Both the history and architecture of the Powhattan House have been considered sufficiently important to make it worthy of preservation, and therefore its plans and photographs of its features have been placed in the Library of Congress by the Historic American Buildings Survey.

The Powhattan House: Galveston's first family hotel

Wilbur F. Cherry House

1602 Church

OUTSTANDING for its simplicity of design is the Cherry house, which with its shady upstairs and downstairs verandas, tall chimneys, and handmade outside boarding gives an impression of strength and comfort which the years have proved well justified. Built between 1852 and 1854, it served the family of Wilbur F. Cherry for some seventy years. During the fire of 1885 it was the only house in its block and one of two in its section of the city to escape injury. It has also successfully weathered every tropical storm that has hit the Island City.

Although the joining of the front and back sections of the house is such as to suggest that the rear ell was an addition, it is actually an integral part of the original structure. Only the railings of the broad galleries have been changed in the course of the years. Iron bolts which run from partitions to corners form part of the substantial and storm-resisting construction of the house. The original floors, which are still in use, were laid with boards of random widths.

The Cherry home is closely connected with the founding of the *Galveston News*. The paper in its first form, under the title simply of the *News,* was established April 11, 1842, by Samuel Bangs—a colorful character who had at one time been a member of the forces of Jean Lafitte—in partnership with his brother-in-law, George H. French. The *News* appeared as a daily for only two months, after which it came off the press only three times a week and then dropped to a weekly schedule.

Meanwhile Wilbur Cherry, the youngest son of Samuel and Abigail Cherry, born in New Haven, New York, in 1820, had come to Texas to help in the fight for its independence. After the Revolution Cherry and Michael Cronican, whom he had met on the battlefield, settled in Galveston and decided to try the newspaper game. Purchasing the *News* from Bangs, they leased his press for $4.00 a month and rented unpretentious quarters on Strand and Tremont Streets for $8.00 monthly. Not long after Bangs left the *News* to sponsor other papers, it was in trouble. Cherry bought Cronican's interest in the paper—in whose title he inserted the word *Galveston*—and felt he had solved his publishing problems by hiring a New York editor. But the editor died before he could begin his work on the paper, and Cherry became desperate in his efforts to continue publication.

Then, in 1843, Cherry brought Willard Richardson to his staff. Richardson soon developed the *News* into the leading newspaper of the state, and in 1845 he bought out Cherry. In 1865 a daily edition was permanently established. That same year Colonel A. H. Belo arrived in Texas from North Carolina and joined the paper's staff. In 1885 the *Galveston News,* under Colonel Belo's leadership, established in the promising town of Dallas a branch publication, the *Dallas Morning News.*

The home which Wilbur Cherry and his wife, Catherine Crosby French, widow of George French, built and in which they lived for many years is now an apartment house, the property of Benjamin Wade.

Not open to visitors.

(Right) Identical upper and lower doorways in Cherry house

(Below) Wilbur F. Cherry house: only the railing of the broad
galleries changed since it was built in 1852-54

Brown Mansion: "Ashton Villa"

2328 Broadway

"ASHTON VILLA," now El Mina Shrine Temple, was built in the 1850's by Captain J. M. Brown. The three-story red brick building, with its ornate wrought-iron decorations, stands in the center of a plot of four city blocks.

Captain Brown, a native of Orange County, New York, moved to Galveston in 1843. Soon he was the owner of the largest wholesale hardware establishment west of New Orleans. He became president of the Galveston Wharf Company, and also of the Galveston, Houston and Henderson Railway Company.

Another of Brown's activities was the operation of a brickyard on Carpenter's Bayou. There are two accounts of the origin of the brick used in his home: that it was brought by schooner from Philadelphia, requiring three months for transportation down the Atlantic Coast and across the Gulf to Galveston; and that it was made by slave labor in Brown's own brickyard.

However that may be, there is no doubt that the Browns, who traveled widely, collected materials and furnishings for their home in many different lands. The delicate wrought iron used in the balcony railings and ornaments and in fences and gates came from England. The walnut valances over the tall windows were carved in Paris, and from that city also came the artisans who decorated the ceilings and walls with friezes, panels, and medallions executed in 22-carat gold leaf. The fine pedestal mirrors, too, are French. The carved newel and handrails of the graceful old staircase were made from imported mahogany.

Because of the massiveness of the house and the height of the ceilings most of the furniture had to be especially designed and built to fit the several rooms. The dining room was spacious enough, and its table large enough, so that forty people might sit down and eat there together.

Miss Betty Brown, Captain Brown's daughter, was not only a Galveston belle, but also an accomplished artist. Her delicately tinted paintings of ladies in flowing robes still hang in the parlor. Off the entrance hall was "Miss Betty's Room," a little alcove which was lined from floor to ceiling with drawers. Here the Captain's daughter stored the art objects and mementoes she collected in her travels around the world.

The grounds around the house, like the interior, showed the family's interest in far places. Many of the shrubs which grew there came from Europe and were set out by Mrs. Brown. Later Captain Brown brought two hundred sparrows from England to protect the plants from insects.

Many elaborate social gatherings were held in the mansion; but it was also the scene of suffering and death when, during the yellow fever epidemic which swept Galveston, it was used as an emergency hospital. Victims of the fever were brought to the house on litters borne by Negro slaves, and Miss Betty and other women of Galveston heroically fought the disease.

The home had its moment, too, of importance in Texas history. Since Galveston was the state's chief port, probably the most important engagements fought in Texas during the Civil War were the taking of the island in 1862 by the Federal forces and its recapture in 1863 by Confederate forces under General John B. Magruder. Both the Union and Confederate commanders used the Brown mansion as headquarters. And on June 18, 1865, the reception room of the house was the scene of the formal end of the war for Texas when the Confederate commanders surrendered their swords to General Gordon Granger, who had come with his troops from New Orleans to receive the surrender of the Trans-Mississippi Department of the Confederate States of America.

In 1928 the Shriners bought the mansion from Mrs. Harry J. Jumonville of New Orleans, a granddaughter of the builder. They made some alterations, removing a few partitions and tearing away the slave quarters to make room for the addition of an assembly hall. But they have preserved most

"Ashton Villa," built in the 1850's by Captain J. M. Brown, now El Mina Shrine Temple;
(above) detail of delicate wrought-iron decoration, and gate and posts, all forged in England

carefully the characteristic decorations of the home, such as the hand-carved valances and mantels. It is fitting that "Ashton Villa" should be the home of El Mina Shrine, for Captain Brown was one of the city's first Masons, and Mrs. Brown was a charter member of the Order of the Eastern Star.

Records of this historically and architecturally famous home have been preserved by the Historic American Buildings Survey.

Open to visitors daily except Sundays; Monday through Friday, 9 a.m. to 12 noon, 1:30 p.m. to 5 p.m.; Saturdays, 9 a.m. to 12 noon.

(Right) Double galleries of the Brown mansion

(Below, left) Walnut frieze, valance, and mirror carved in France

(Below, right) Ceiling medallion of 22-carat gold leaf made by artisans brought from France